super smoothies

maggie's centre
cancer caring centre

BOOK REVIEW
We would appreciate your comments
about this book and a rating from
1-5 (1 = poor, 5 = excellent)

DEMCO

50 RECIPES
FOR HEALTH AND
ENERGY

super
smoothies

MARY CORPENING BARBER AND SARA CORPENING WHITEFORD

PHOTOGRAPHS BY E. J. ARMSTRONG

CHRONICLE BOOKS

SAN FRANCISCO

Library of Congress Cataloging-in-Publication Data:
Barber, Mary Corpening, 1969–
Super smoothies: 50 recipes for health and energy/
by Mary Corpening Barber and Sara Corpening Whiteford;
photographs by E. J. Armstrong.
    p. cm.
Includes index.
ISBN 0-8118-2540-X (pbk.)
1. Fruit drinks. 2. Smoothies (Beverages)
I. Corpening Whiteford, Sara, 1969– II. Title
TX815 .B38 2000
641.8'75—dc21   99-39549
                              CIP

Manufactured in China.

Prop styling by Patty Whittmann
Food styling by Kim Holderman
Designed by Elizabeth Van Itallie

Distributed in Canada by Raincoast Books
9050 Shaughnessy Street
Vancouver, British Columbia V6P 6E5

10 9 8 7

Chronicle Books LLC
85 Second Street
San Francisco, California 94105

www.chroniclebooks.com

acknowledgments

Our sincere thanks to Alison Horton Eastwood, whose expertise in the realm of nutrition was the guiding force behind this book. Her dedication, persistence, and professionalism added tremendous value to this project.

Many, many, thanks to Jan Newbury, who provided profound insights and fabulous advice along the way. We are grateful for her coherent compilation of the text and her flair for expression. She has captured our enthusiasm for smoothie making, which was one of our main objectives for this book.

Thanks to Erik and Jack, our loving husbands, who, whether they know it or not, are our most valued tasters.

An extremely heartfelt appreciation to all our recipe testers: Victoria Reid, Katrina Martelino, Patricia Willets, Andrea Cardoso, Deli Haynes, Lila Rifaat, Lucy Bowen Taylor, and last but not least, baby Jackson Barber!

As always, thanks to Jane Dystel, our insightful agent, and to Bill LeBlond and the gang at Chronicle Books, for helping to shape *Super Smoothies*. It was a thrill to be involved in such an exciting project.

contents

introduction

Everybody loves smoothies. It's no surprise. They are a cinch to make and require little equipment—a knife, a blender, and a few high-quality ingredients. They're chock-full of nutrients, and though most are low to moderate in calories and fat, smoothies are right off the Richter scale when it comes to taste. It's no wonder that the demand for them is insatiable. But smoothie heads have begun to demand more from their favorite drinks than just great flavor. They now insist on power drinks custom-blended for individual health needs. Check the menu at your local smoothie shack. Where you used to see a listing of fun fruit drinks, you'll find smoothies that claim to cure your cold, boost your immune system, and pump you up for a power workout. The evidence is in, and it's clear that smoothies offer an extraordinary nutritional experience. Made with enticing fresh fruits and vegetables, these popular drinks offer a delicious and convenient way to get all the vital nutrients necessary for good health.

In *Super Smoothies,* we've taken advantage of the tremendous amount of recent nutritional research to make drinks that may help you sleep, ward off a cold, or calm an upset stomach. A registered dietitian has analyzed every recipe in this book and offered advice on how to combine ingredients to get the maximum benefit from each healthy, flavorful drink. We have smoothies that can fuel a workout, freshen up your breath, and may even help enhance your love life.

The fifty super-charged smoothie recipes in this book were developed with the well-being of the entire family in mind. Pregnant women, the weight conscious, and even teething babies can benefit from the nutritionally enhanced fresh-fruit blends included here.

Though all the smoothies in this book were developed with the goal of promoting good health, the most important requirement we had for every recipe was that it taste great. No smoothie, no matter how healthy it may be, will do much good if you don't want to drink it. In this book, flavor always comes first. We left out taste- and texture-altering nutritional supplements of dubious value and relied instead on peak-of-the-season produce and other flavorful ingredients. In the pages ahead you'll find recipes for fifty absolutely irresistible smoothies that will nourish your mind, body, and soul.

So plug in your blender and drink to your health. Super Smoothies are here.

ten tips for
super smoothies

1. The very best smoothies are made from the highest-quality fruit. For the most flavorful smoothies, always use perfectly ripe fruit in the prime of its season. Also, use organic fruit whenever possible.

2. A smoothie is only as good as the sum of its parts. Use all natural ingredients, if possible. Avoid artificial ingredients and sweeteners such as aspartame (which is often inconspicuously labeled) and NutraSweet, which can leave an unpleasant aftertaste.

3. Use fresh frozen fruits within two weeks. Their flavor fades the longer they stay in the freezer. If your frozen fruit is freezer-burned, rinse it with cold water to avoid an unpleasant aftertaste. Also, scrape any freezer burn from sorbets or frozen yogurts before adding to smoothies.

4. Experiment with flavored ice cubes. This is a great way to create a cool and thick smoothie, full of concentrated flavor. To make, simply pour the juice, tea, or nectar of your preference into an ice cube tray and freeze.

5. For the best consistency, use very small ice cubes or crushed ice. Though blender manufacturers advertise that their machines can pulverize ice cubes, no matter what their size, this is not always the case. For best results, always crush ice before putting it into a blender. Put ice cubes in a strong self-sealing plastic bag, remove excess air, and place the bag on a firm surface such as a counter. Smash the cubes with a rolling pin or a heavy metal pan until crushed.

6. For a thick, dense smoothie, add an extra handful of frozen fruit, crushed ice, or frozen yogurt or sorbet. If you prefer a thinner, lighter consistency, simply add more liquid. At different times during the day, we prefer different textures and temperatures. Use these recipes as guidelines and adjust them to suit your own taste.

7. It's our opinion that the very best-tasting smoothies are additive free. We find that nutritional supplements compete with the pure fresh taste and smooth texture of a smoothie. If you are adamant about using additives, try adding them to a small portion of the smoothie so you can enjoy the remainder in its pure, delicious state.

8. If your smoothie is not sweet enough, due to the sugar content of the fruit, add a bit of honey, maple syrup, barley malt, brown rice syrup, stevia (a sweet-tasting plant extract), or another natural sweetener. Half of a very ripe banana is another way to make a smoothie sweeter.

9. We prefer low-fat dairy products in our smoothies. They help us keep calories and fat at a minimum and still taste great. But nonfat dairy products may be substituted in any of the recipes in this book.

10. No smoothie is ever better than in the first few minutes after it's made. For the best possible flavor and texture, drink them right away. If you must make them ahead, you'll notice that some smoothies begin to separate after 20 minutes. If that happens, simply stir it or put the smoothie back into the blender for a minute to bring it back to its original consistency.

fruit glossary

APPLES The crisp, tart taste of an apple can add a lot to a smoothie. We sometimes add peeled or unpeeled cubes of apples, and other times we use juice, concentrate, or cider, and sometimes applesauce. Though not particularly rich in vitamins, other than a little vitamin C, apples do contain high levels of pectin that can help reduce cholesterol levels. When buying juice and applesauce, check to be sure that they contain no artificial sweeteners or flavorings.

APRICOTS Pale orange apricots with a slight pink blush look like plump baby cheeks. We think they're one of the prettiest fruits around. They also happen to be a powerhouse of beta-carotene, an antioxidant that's essential for vision, growth, reproduction, and a sound immune system. Apricots are also a good source of potassium and fiber and are rich in cancer-fighting antioxidants. In the summer when apricots are in season, we use fresh ones in our smoothies. The rest of the year we rely on canned apricots, apricot nectar, or dried apricots, which can be reconstituted and added to smoothies. Dried apricots are one of the most concentrated sources of beta-carotene available and an excellent source of iron.

BANANAS It's hard to imagine what smoothies would be without bananas. They are used more often than any other fruit, lending not only flavor, but also the characteristic creamy texture that gives smoothies their name. They are a fantastic source of potassium, an electrolyte often lost during exercise, as well as magnesium, folate, and vitamin B6, which may decrease the risk of heart disease. Buy them at any stage and let them ripen at home.

BLACKBERRIES You may love these luscious dark berries for their sweet, juicy taste, but nutrition researchers value them for the role they may play in preventing heart disease and reducing high blood pressure. They are rich in antioxidants, potassium, and compounds known as saponins, all key nutrients for a healthy heart. You'll find fresh black-berries in the market in July and August. Look for plump berries with a

FRUITS

deep black color. Blackberries with their green hulls attached may look pretty, but were likely picked too soon and may be overly tart. Frozen unsweetened ones, a good choice for smoothies, are available all year round. The tiny blackberry seeds can be a nuisance, so you may want to pour your blackberry smoothies through a strainer.

BLUEBERRIES We used to think of blueberries as quaint little fruits to add to muffins and sprinkle over cereal, but we've learned that these innocent-looking berries have one of the highest known antioxidant levels of any fruit. That means that blueberries may help protect against cancer, eye conditions, and some of the problems that accompany aging. They are also one of the best sources of salicylate, a natural aspirinlike compound that has been shown to reduce inflammation. You'll find them fresh in the markets in the late spring when blue-berries are at their peak, but these fruits freeze well, too, so you can use them in smoothies any time of the year. You can also buy frozen unsweetened blueberries.

CANTALOUPE Orange-fleshed cantaloupe is one of the best nutri-tional buys in the fruit world. Half an average melon provides more than the daily requirement for vitamins A and C, and less than 100 calories. Cantaloupe is also an excellent source of potassium, which aids in regulating the exchange of nutrients between cells. You'll find these miracle melons in the market during the summer months. The best ones have a thick, close netting on the rind, yield gently to pressure, and have a fruity aroma.

CHERRIES Almost everyone loves cherries, but folks who work out regularly can appreciate this fruit for more than just its great taste. Cherries are rich in potassium and the B vitamins, as well as A and C. They also contain anthocyanins, which are antioxidants that may protect against some types of cancer. Cherries are available in a wide range of color, from extra-large and black (Bing) to large and yellow-red (Royal Anne) to smaller and red (Lamberts). All of these sweet cherries make wonderful smoothies. Be sure to remove the pits and stems before you add cherries to the blender. You can extend their short season by freez-ing cherries in self-sealing plastic bags.

CRANBERRIES For years, women have told one another about the wonders that cranberry juice can do in relieving bladder infections. It turns out that there is more than anecdote to support this recommendation. Researchers have discovered an as yet unnamed compound in cranberries that prevents bacteria from attaching to the bladder and can aid in washing out the pathogens that cause infections. Stock up on fresh cranberries when they're available during the holiday season, and freeze them to use all year round.

DATES Calcium, magnesium, fiber, and folate are some of the great reasons to love dates, but the truth is we add them to smoothies because they taste good. They're also a wonderful source of iron, a particularly important mineral for women. You can find dates in the dried fruit section of your market all year round. Just remember to remove the pits, or you could damage your blender. Dates tend to dry out when not stored properly and can be difficult to blend. If the ones you have on hand have hardened, pour boiling water over them, cover, and let stand for 15 minutes before draining.

GRAPEFRUIT While most everyone loves the tart, sweet taste of grapefruit, those who are at risk of heart disease can appreciate them for more than just their flavor. In fact, they might look at a grapefruit as a heart pill with a rind. These popular citrus fruits contain vitamin C, which can help stabilize plaque lesions in arteries, and pectin, which can reduce cholesterol levels. They also contain potassium, which helps to combat high blood pressure. They are also a source of antioxidants that may prevent some cancers, and folate, an important compound for preventing birth defects. Pick a pink grapefruit and you'll get a dose of beta-carotene as well. Both grapefruit juice and seeded sections can go into the blender for making smoothies. If you're using fresh grapefruit, take extra care to remove all the white pith. Despite the fact that it's nutrient-rich, it has a bitter taste that can ruin a smoothie.

GRAPES (GREEN) Big bunches of green grapes are one of our favorite snacks. They're also a part of some of our favorite smoothies. These little green gems are a good source of vitamin C, an important antioxidant, and potassium, an important mineral that contributes to a healthy nervous system and a regular heart rhythm.

seasonal fruit chart

SPRING	SUMMER	AUTUMN	WINTER
(mid-March to mid-June)	(mid-June to mid-September)	(mid-September to mid-December)	(mid-December to mid-March)
blueberries	apricots	apples	bananas
strawberries	blackberries	cranberries	dried fruits
	cantaloupe	dates	grapefruit
	cherries `	pears	kiwis
	grapes		oranges
	honeydew		pineapple
	litchi nuts		
	mangos		
	nectarines		
	papayas		
	peaches		
	plums		
	raspberries		
	watermelon		

GRAPES (RED)   We've all heard the news that red wine can protect against heart disease. Well, the same chemical, called resveratrol, is found in red grapes, which means that those who want to avoid the negative effects of alcohol can still benefit from some of the good things wine has to offer. Red grapes also offer a good dose of potassium, which contributes to a healthy nervous system and a regular heart rhythm. Grape juice and concentrate offer the same benefits.

GUAVA NECTAR   Soft, seductive guavas are one of the more luscious fruits we know, but unfortunately they can be hard to come by. Luckily, we can always get our hands on guava nectar. Its rich perfume and exotic tutti-frutti flavor make a wonderful addition to a smoothie. Guavas are an excellent source of beta-carotene, which promotes good vision and helps maintain healthy skin, and vitamin C, which contributes to healthy gums and teeth and aids in the healing of wounds.

HONEYDEW MELON   The subtle, sweet flavor of these pale green melons is one we never tire of, and their dense, creamy flesh is perfect for smoothies. Ripe honeydew is perhaps the sweetest of melons. It's a terrific low-calorie addition to a smoothie and a good source of potassium and vitamin C.

FRUITS

KIWIS These oversized berries are something of a diamond in the rough. Their fuzzy brown peel offers no clue to the jewel-like fruit that lies just beyond it. Slice one in half and you'll reveal a starburst of emerald green flesh surrounded by a ring of black seeds. Just one of these fruits has twice the vitamin C of an orange. They have relatively few calories and are a good source of potassium and fiber. Those seeds that give the fruit such a distinctive look can give a smoothie a bitter taste and odd texture if ground up in a blender. We've found that a food processor leaves the seeds intact, and we recommend always using one instead of a blender when making smoothies with kiwis.

LEMON JUICE Sometimes a sweet, fruity smoothie just begs for a little bit of acid to balance the flavor. That's when we reach for the lemons. Like all citrus, lemons are bursting with vitamin C. The fresher the lemon juice, the better it tastes.

LIME JUICE The lemon's little green cousin first gained nutritional fame as a cure for scurvy. Today limes, and other citrus too, are heralded for their disease-fighting antioxidants and the cholesterol-lowering pectin of their flesh. The bright taste of fresh lime juice is sometimes all that's needed to bring an overly sweet smoothie into line.

LITCHI NUTS If you've never tasted litchi nuts, get ready to be wowed. They have a glorious perfume and a sweet floral flavor that make for a heavenly smoothie. These magnificent Chinese fruits are an excellent source of vitamin C and are rich in potassium, too.

MANGOS The lovely yellow-orange flesh of a mango indicates that it is a rich source of beta-carotene. These tropical fruits also contain potassium, as well as vitamin C, the nutrient that can give a boost to an ailing immune system and help protect an ailing heart. A mango's creamy texture is ideal for making smoothies, and you can find mangos in the market most any time of the year. To choose a ripe one, press gently against the flesh. It should feel subtly soft. Another test for ripeness is to hold the fruit up to your nose and breathe deeply. Those with no scent are not ready to eat, and ones that smell sour are past their prime, but if you smell a sweet, fruity perfume, take the fruit home and enjoy a mango at its peak.

NECTARINES Some folks think of nectarines as peaches without the fuzz. Although their flavor is similar, nectarines have somewhat firmer flesh, and nutritionally speaking, they are even richer in the antioxidants that bolster the immune system. They're also an excellent source of vitamin C.

ORANGES Everyone knows that oranges are a good source of vitamin C and are often recommended to fight colds. But not everyone realizes that vitamin C is an antioxidant that strengthens the immune system. Oranges also contain pectin, which may reduce cholesterol levels and decrease the risk of cancer. They are also an excellent source of folate, which is an important nutrient for pregnant women. Folate can also help lower elevated homocysteine levels, possibly reducing cardiovascular risk. Note that women at risk of osteoporosis can appreciate the added benefits of calcium-fortified orange juice. If you're looking for a quick substitute for fresh orange segments, use canned mandarin oranges instead.

PAPAYAS The orange fruit tinged with pink is a dead giveaway to a papaya's beta-carotene content. These smooth-fleshed tropical fruits also contain antioxidants, which can promote a healthy immune system, and an enzyme that aids in digestion. You'll also get a dose of vitamin C and fiber when you add papaya to a smoothie. Its creamy texture makes for a lusciously rich-tasting drink.

PEACHES Like other orange-fleshed fruits and vegetables, peaches are rich in beta-carotene. They also contain vitamin C and potassium; all of these work together to aid in the fight against cancer, heart disease, and strokes, and may even improve memory and protect against some of the negative effects of aging. Fresh, frozen, or canned in their own juices, peaches can bring flavor and texture to smoothies all year round.

PEARS The intense flavor and heady perfume of a fresh, ripe pear are hard to resist. But pears have a lot more going for them than just flavor. Like other fruits, pears are a good source of fiber and energy-giving carbohydrates. Pear nectar offers all the great taste and health benefits of a fresh pear without the bother of cutting and peeling the fruit.

FRUITS

PINEAPPLE There's something about pineapple smoothies that makes us want to drop a paper umbrella in the glass and go sit on a beach towel. The citrusy, sweet-tart taste of pineapple makes it one of our favorite smoothie ingredients. Pineapple smoothies can help soothe a sore throat and ease the pain of inflamed gums. They are also a good source of vitamin C and potassium. To pick a ripe pineapple, look for a sweet, aromatic smell. Another clue is to tug on a leaf. If it comes off easily the fruit is usually ripe and ready to eat.

PLUMS There are literally hundreds of varieties of plums, and we've never met one we didn't like. Their tart, sweet taste is perfect for an icy cold smoothie on a hot afternoon. Plums are rich in vitamin C, an antioxidant that can help stall some of the effects of aging. They are also a source of potassium, a mineral that may help reduce high blood pressure.

PRUNES These tasty dried plums are the butt of a lot of bad jokes, but the truth is that they are an absolutely delicious dried fruit. Along with their well-known stores of fiber, prunes are also an excellent source of beta-carotene, iron, potassium, and vitamin C. If your prunes seem particularly firm, you may want to rehydrate them in boiling water for 10 minutes. Drain before putting them in the blender.

RASPBERRIES For most of our lives, we've loved raspberries just for their sweet taste. Then we started researching this book and learned that there's more to these beautiful berries than wonderful flavor. High levels of potassium make raspberries a terrific food to enjoy after a trip to the gym, where we often deplete our store of this important nutrient. Raspberries are also loaded with salicylates, a compound that has been shown to reduce inflammation, and are a good source of vitamin B6 and magnesium. Because they freeze well, these summer berries can be used in smoothies all year round. You can also buy frozen unsweetened raspberries.

STRAWBERRIES A juicy red strawberry is surely one of nature's greatest achievements. Not only do they have a wonderful flavor, they also pack a whole lot of nutritional value into a little bitty berry. Strawberries are a rich source of vitamin C, and like a lot of other berries, they are high in disease-fighting phytochemicals. Though you can now find fresh strawberries all year round, they are never better than in the late spring. Choose those with a heady perfume, the best indication of flavor, or buy frozen unsweetened ones to use any time. Strawberry nectar is another wonderful way to get that great berry taste into your blender.

WATERMELON It's the water that makes this bright red-fleshed melon such a good choice for an after-workout smoothie or for any other time you might be dehydrated. Rich in the electrolytes that are lost during exercise, watermelons are nature's Gatorade. They are also a good source of vitamin C and may protect against some cancers.

vegetable glossary

AVOCADOS Nothing quite matches the subtle nutlike flavor and buttery, smooth texture of a ripe avocado. Though they pack a lot of calories, avocados are an excellent source of monounsaturated fats, the same type of fat that's found in olive oil and has been associated with lower rates of heart disease. Avocados are also rich in vitamin E, which may help men increase their fertility rate, and folate, a vitamin that pregnant women need to prevent birth defects. Their generous stores of potassium may help to reduce high blood pressure.

BEETS A sugar-sweet flavor and vivid red color make beets a fantastic addition to savory smoothies. Nutritionally speaking, we've discovered that beets are loaded with antioxidants that can help rejuvenate just about every bodily organ and system. We love them, too, as a source of vitamin C and folate.

CARROTS When we were kids, our folks always told us that carrots could help improve our eyesight. No one mentioned that they might also protect us from cancer and reduce the risk of heart disease. They are also chock-full of carotenoids, which help fight disease. It wouldn't have made any difference, though; we ate our carrots anyway, just because we

V E G E T A B L E S

liked the taste. When making smoothies, we sometimes buy fresh carrot juice at the natural foods store or juice bar, or just grate fresh carrots right into the blender.

CUCUMBER Low in calories and full of hydrating water, cucumbers are one of the most refreshing vegetables we know. It's not necessary to peel cucumbers for smoothies, but we do recommend that you buy organic, unwaxed varieties or English hothouse cucumbers, as pesticides may be sealed in the wax used to coat cucumbers.

RED BELL PEPPERS Most red and orange fruits and vegetables are excellent sources of beta-carotene and vitamin C. Red bell peppers are no exception. Adding them to your diet can bolster your immune system and help to fight infection and disease.

TOMATOES Ripe red tomatoes still warm from the sun say summer in a way that few other foods can. We love them in savory smoothies for lunch on busy days. Tomatoes offer a megadose of vitamin C and are a good source of cancer-fighting antioxidants, such as lycopene. Rich in potassium and magnesium, too, they are a good choice for post-workout smoothies, when those minerals may need to be restored. There is some evidence that the body absorbs the nutrients in tomatoes best when the vegetables are finely chopped, pureed, or cooked (as canned tomatoes and tomato juice are)—good news for tomato-smoothie fans. Enjoy fresh tomatoes all summer long when they are at their flavorful (and nutritional) best. The supermarket tomatoes available the rest of the year have the taste and texture of a ball of yarn. Rely on canned tomatoes, tomato juice, or even tomato paste when the summer season comes to an end.

the scoop on binders and other secret ingredients

ALMOND MILK Not really milk at all, almond milk is a blend of crushed almonds and water and has a delicate, slightly sweet flavor that tastes great in a smoothie. You can find it in natural foods stores as well as many supermarkets. Almond milk is relatively low in fat and it has no cholesterol. It is a good alternative for anyone who has trouble digesting cow's milk.

ALMONDS We sometimes throw a handful of toasted almonds into the blender when we're making smoothies. They are a powerhouse of protein as well as a top source of disease-fighting antioxidants. Like other nuts, almonds are rich in iron, magnesium, fiber, protein, zinc, calcium, vitamin E, folate, niacin, phosphorus, potassium, and riboflavin. These energy-rich minerals can protect against the effects of fatigue and stress.

BRAN Some foods suffer from a reputation for being almost too nutritious. Take bran, for instance. We love its sweet, nutty taste, but we sometimes have a hard time convincing people that it's not just another good-for-you-so-it-must-taste-bad kind of food. Bran is simply the outer layer of a grain, such as wheat or oats, which is removed in the milling process. An excellent source of fiber, bran makes an excellent addition to a smoothie, but keep in mind that it can change the texture, so don't overdo it.

BUTTERMILK We're always surprised when we see the words "low-fat" on the label of the buttermilk carton. It tastes so creamy and rich we're certain it must be loaded with fat, but the truth is that buttermilk is not only low in fat, it's a terrific source of protein and calcium, perfect for growing kids and adults, too.

COCONUT MILK Don't confuse coconut milk with sweetened "cream of coconut," which is chock-full of sugar and artificial ingredients.

BINDERS

Coconut milk is very high in saturated fat, so instead use light coconut milk, which contains as much as 60 percent less fat and still adds a creamy, rich texture to smoothies. Don't worry if the milk has a lumpy texture—just stir to dissolve these lumps of solidified coconut cream.

FLAXSEED AND FLAXSEED OIL There's just too much good stuff in these little seeds not to add them to smoothies now and then. Flaxseed is a rich source of omega-3 essential fatty acids, the famed "good" fat that's found in fish and is believed to prevent harmful cholesterol from depositing into the arteries, leading to heart disease. These omega-3 fats benefit brain growth and development and may help to prevent irregular heartbeat, too. Flaxseed also contains antioxidants and plant estrogens that may reduce cancer risk. It's also an excellent source of fiber. See, we told you it was good. You can find both the seeds and oil at natural foods stores. Whole flaxseed must be ground to release its essential oils. You can do this in a coffee or spice grinder. Be sure to refrigerate or freeze the ground flaxseed to prevent it from going rancid. Flaxseed oil should be refrigerated as well.

GINGER The fresh, spicy taste of ginger is a terrific accent to all sorts of fruit. Intake can act as a digestive aid, as well as a preventative of motion sickness. Pregnant women and anyone prone to motion sickness can benefit from ginger's ability to suppress nausea. Everyone else can just enjoy the great taste.

HONEY Sometimes a smoothie, particularly ones made with lots of tart citrus fruit, needs a little sweetener to balance out the flavor. That's when we reach for the honey. Because it's sweeter than white sugar, a little honey can go a long way. One word of warning, though: Honey can transmit botulism, even when pasteurized, and so should never be given to infants under the age of one. As an alternative, try other natural sweeteners such as barley malt, brown rice syrup, or stevia (an herbal sweetener), all of which can be found at natural foods stores.

MAPLE SYRUP If you've never tasted real maple syrup, you're in for a treat. No, we're not talking about pancake syrup, that bland mixture of corn syrup and artificial flavorings that is so cloying it makes our teeth ache just to think about it. Real maple syrup is subtle and full of rich, complex flavors that no imitation comes close to duplicating. When shopping for maple syrup, look for one labeled "Grade A Dark Amber." It will have a richer maple flavor than the more expensive, lighter-tasting Fancy grade syrup. And if you're lucky enough to find some Grade B maple syrup, snap it up. It has the most intense maple flavor of all the commercially available maple syrups. Maple syrup is a wonderful alternative sweetener that adds a real depth of flavor to smoothies.

MILK Got milk? We always do. It's one of those nutrient-packed foods that we can't live without. Milk provides nearly all the substances essential for good health. It's loaded with protein, calcium, Vitamin D, riboflavin, and other vitamins and minerals as well. Though milk does have some drawbacks, most notably the saturated fat and cholesterol found in whole milk, these can be avoided by using low-fat or nonfat milk. We sometimes use powdered dry milk for smoothies when we want to boost the calcium content without adding more liquid. Low-fat evaporated milk (not nonfat, which is too thin and lacks flavor) makes a super-rich smoothie without much fat.

MINT There's something so fresh and candylike about mint. We love the way a fresh sprig or two can add another dimension to the fruity taste of our favorite smoothies. But mint is more than just a great flavor. It is also a digestive that can help prevent nausea and morning sickness in pregnant women.

PEANUT BUTTER We've never outgrown the taste of peanut butter, and we're happy to report that there's no reason why anyone should. Not only is it a great source of cholesterol-free protein (peanuts have more protein than any other nut), but peanut butter is also chock-full of heart-healthy mono-unsaturated and polyunsaturated fats. It also contains the same substance found in red wine that may reduce the incidence of heart disease. There's a lot of other goodness in peanut butter, too, like potassium, fiber, vitamin E, folate, iron, magnesium, niacin, and phosphorus.

PUMPKIN SEEDS When we were little kids, we used to save the seeds from our jack-o-lanterns to toast and eat as a snack. Now, we enjoy pump-

BINDERS

kin seeds all year round and often add them to our smoothies. They're a nutritional powerhouse, loaded with iron and protein, which is a lot more than you can say about the bags of candy we collected every year.

RED WINE   All too often, nutritionists are telling us why the things that we enjoy the most are bad for us, so we were delighted to learn that there are in fact some benefits from a diet that includes a moderate amount of red wine. Research indicates that red wine may reduce the risk of heart disease and help keep coronary arteries from becoming clogged. Now, that's news we can drink to.

RICE MILK   A low-fat, creamy alternative to cow's milk, rice milk offers variety for lactose-intolerant smoothie-lovers and people looking to reduce the amount of fat in their diet. Choose enriched rice milk, with vitamins D, E, and A or beta-carotene added, and a calcium content similar to that of cow's milk, to make sure that you get your fill of these important nutrients. Because rice milk has a fairly sweet taste, you may want to cut back on any other sweeteners when using it.

SOFT SILKEN TOFU   This particular type of tofu can make a mean smoothie—rich and creamy and loaded with nutrients. Tofu is an excellent source of cholesterol-free protein, is low in sodium, and is absolutely teeming with phytoestrogens, which may protect against some cancers and heart disease, bring relief from some of the uncomfortable symptoms of menopause, and protect against osteoporosis. Soft silken tofu has just the right texture for smoothies; no other kind will blend as smoothly. Most often, soft silken tofu is found in packages in the refrigerated section of supermarkets, but some brands are found in the dry-goods section.

SOY MILK   Soy milk is absolutely jammed with wonderful stuff, like protein and antioxidants that protect against disease and aging. We like cow's milk with our cookies and chocolate cake, but soy milk is terrific when blended in a smoothie where fruit takes center stage. Available in a range of flavors, our favorite soy milk is the rich-tasting vanilla version. Some producers offer fortified soy milk that's enriched with beta-carotene, vitamin B12, calcium, and vitamin E. Soy is also a great substitute for those who are lactose intolerant or have a milk allergy.

SUNFLOWER SEEDS For years, we've enjoyed sunflower seeds as a snack. They have a wonderful fresh, nutty flavor that tastes great in a smoothie, too. Like other nuts and seeds, they are a good source of the protein necessary for building and repairing cells. They are also rich in fatty acids and fiber, which may reduce cholesterol levels, and are a good source of vitamin E, calcium, folate, thiamin, and B6.

TAHINI This rich sesame seed paste adds a whole new dimension of flavor to a smoothie, particularly when paired with bananas. There are substances in sesame seeds that may protect against some cancers and inhibit the growth of tumors. These tiny seeds are also full of calcium (ten times as much as in an equal weight of milk!) and are a highly efficient source of cholesterol-free protein.

TEA There are few things in life as soothing as a cup of tea. One of them is a smoothie made with tea. But tea has more to offer than just comfort. It's rich in a variety of antioxidants that may prevent cancer and inhibit all sorts of viruses. It is also a natural source of fluoride and may protect teeth against the bacteria that cause cavities. And because tea contains caffeine, which is a stimulant, tea-based smoothies may actually enhance a workout.

VANILLA EXTRACT There's nothing plain about vanilla. We think it's one of the most delicious flavors on the planet. Just a bit of vanilla extract can bring out all the rich fruit flavors of a smoothie, and it just may improve your love life, as well. There's some indication that pure vanilla extract can stimulate the motor nerves used in sexual response.

YOGURT The tart taste of yogurt makes it one of our favorite smoothie ingredients. We use both frozen yogurt and fresh yogurt and take advantage of the full range of flavors available. The bacteria that gives fresh yogurt its tang also promotes the growth of healthy bacteria and stimulates the immune system to help ailing bodies fight disease. (Note that freezing kills this bacteria, so frozen yogurt, though delicious, is not as nutritious as fresh.) And yogurt is rich in all sorts of nutrients, such as protein, calcium, magnesium, zinc, and riboflavin, as well.

BINDERS

glossary

building blocks
for sound nutrition

As you use the recipes in this book, it's important to understand some of the building blocks of sound nutrition basics. Here is a list of some of the essential nutrients and the role they play in a healthy diet.

BETA-CAROTENE Beta-carotene is only one carotenoid out of hundreds that act as antioxidants in disease prevention. When you consume a fruit or vegetable that is beta-carotene rich, you're getting a dose of a multitude of disease-fighting carotenoids such as alpha-carotene, beta-cryptokanthin, lutein, and lycopene (which has been linked to combating prostate cancer). So eat up! No Recommended Daily Allowance (RDA) has been established for the orange-colored fruits and vegetables that are rich in this antioxidant, but the intake recommended by nutrition experts is 5 to 6 milligrams daily.

CALCIUM We could never understand why Mom made such a big deal about us drinking our milk. Then we learned that milk and other dairy products are rich in calcium, the mineral responsible for strong bones. Calcium also regulates heartbeat and muscle contractions. It's essential for blood clotting, and may also help prevent hypertension. Good sources are cow's milk, and fortified soy milk and orange juice. The Dietary Reference Intake (DRI), which is a new set of guidelines for optimal health and prevention of chronic disease, is 1,000 mg of calcium a day for 19- to 50-year-olds, and 1,200 mg a day for those over 50.

CARBOHYDRATES This is the basic nutrient that provides the body with energy. It provides the energy that gets you through the day. Fruits and vegetables, the main ingredients of most smoothies, are both excellent sources of these essential energizers. It is recommended that one get at least 55 to 65 percent of total daily calories from carbohydrates. For example, the average person with an intake of 2,000 calories daily would want to intake approximately 275 to 325 grams of carbohydrates daily to meet the recommended daily calories from carbohydrates.

FAT Despite its bad rap, fat is absolutely essential to good health. It transports fat-soluble vitamins, helps form cell membranes, insulates internal organs, is essential for the manufacture of hormones, and aids the immune system. It is also the most concentrated source of dietary energy. Because excessive fat intake is linked to obesity and many diseases, it's recommended that we limit the amount of fat we eat to approximately 40 to 60 grams daily (20 percent or less of total calories should be coming from fat). To figure out the maximum number of fat grams that you should intake daily, simply take 20 percent of your approximate daily calorie intake and divide by 9. Smoothies get most of their fat content from milk, yogurt, soy products, and nuts. Be aware that saturated fat and cholesterol is what contributes to hardening of arteries or heart disease.

FIBER Fruits and vegetables are an excellent source of fiber, which delivers the bulk that keeps the intestines running smoothly. Fiber also works like a sponge, absorbing toxic substances and preventing them from entering the bloodstream. The recommended intake is 25 to 35 grams daily. Dates, prunes, flaxseed powder, and bran are particularly fiber rich.

FOLATE Folate is a B vitamin that helps prevent birth defects as well as heart disease. It is very important for pregnant women to have a diet that is rich in folate, which is necessary for normal development of the baby's nervous system (especially before conception and during the first six weeks of pregnancy). Orange juice, wheat germ, and brewer's yeast in smoothies are great dietary sources of folate. The RDA is 400 mcg (micrograms).

IRON This mineral, vital for strong blood, is what gives blood its red color. Iron gets so much attention because it is one of the most common nutritional deficiencies in the world. For a reliable remedy, combine a good source of vitamin C (citrus fruits, berries, fortified orange juice) with iron-rich *Super Smoothies* ingredients (avocado, apricots, soy milk, tofu) to enhance iron's absorption. The RDA is 15 mg.

MAGNESIUM This mineral is involved in over three hundred metabolic reactions in the body. It also promotes bone growth and aids nerve, bone, and muscle function. A low intake of magnesium has been associated with irregular heartbeat and high blood pressure. Avocado, bananas, dates, kiwis, and prunes all contain magnesium. The RDA is 400 mg.

PHOSPHORUS This mineral works with calcium in forming bones and teeth, and it also makes up cell membranes and genetic material. One of its most important functions is to help metabolize food, thus releasing energy. For a boost in this important mineral, drink smoothies with nuts and dairy. The RDA is 1,200 mg.

PHYTOCHEMICALS This big word has a simple definition: It simply means plant chemicals. Phytochemicals are not vitamins or minerals, but biologically active substances that protect us from such chronic diseases as cancer and heart disease and are thought to stimulate immune function. The following are examples of phytochemicals and their food sources: isoflavones in soy foods and flaxseed; polyphenols in green tea, grapes, red wine, grape juice, and berries; lycopene in tomatoes, watermelon, apricots, pink grapefruit, and guava; terpenes in cherries and citrus peel; and phenolic acids in tomatoes, citrus fruit, carrots, whole grains, and nuts. Currently there is no RDA for phytochemicals, but nutrition experts recommend eating a minimum of five servings of fruits and vegetables daily for a good amount of phytochemicals (a medium piece of fruit or vegetable or ½ cup cooked or sliced fruit or vegetable equals one serving).

POTASSIUM Healthy hearts and nervous systems depend on potassium to keep them running right. Adequate intake of this mineral (3,000 mg daily) may even help to prevent stroke as it can help maintain stable blood pressure. Exercise can deplete stores of potassium, an electrolyte, which is often lost during a workout. Many smoothies are rich in potassium, especially those made with apricots, bananas, orange juice, and avocados.

PROTEIN Without protein, the body would cease many of its vital functions, including blood clotting, repairing cells, and producing essential enzymes. Smoothies get the bulk of their protein from the addition of milk or yogurt. Soy products, such as tofu, soy milk, and nuts also add protein to our favorite drinks. The RDA of protein for women is about 50 grams and for men about 60 grams.

SELENIUM This trace mineral is an antioxidant that provides protection to the immune system and may help prevent certain types of tumors. Healthy hearts and livers depend on selenium for proper maintenance and function. The selenium content of foods varies widely, because it depends on the selenium of the soil in which the food was grown. Adding bran to a smoothie is one way to boost its selenium content. The RDA is 55 mcg (micrograms) for women and 75 mcg for men. Most health professionals recommend between 100 and 200 mcg for its antioxidant effects.

SODIUM Proper water balance and blood pH levels depend on proper levels of sodium in the body. Athletes and people who are active can lose significant amounts of sodium through perspiration and it is necessary to replenish the lost salt. Most of us have plenty, if not too much, sodium in our systems. Smoothies are naturally low in sodium, although a pinch of salt in some smoothies, particularly ones made with melon, can really enhance the taste. A RDA hasn't been established; however, nutrition experts and various health organizations recommend an intake of no more than 2,400 mg daily, which would be approximately 1 teaspoon salt.

VITAMIN A Healthy skin and good vision are just a few benefits of vitamin A. It also helps maintain the mucus membranes, the body's first line of defense against toxic invaders. Beta-carotene, an antioxidant found in orange and red-fleshed fruits and vegetables, is converted by the body into vitamin A and may play an important role in cancer prevention. It may also reduce the risk of heart disease. Growth and reproductive systems also depend on vitamin A. Make a smoothie with carrots, cantaloupes, apricots, or peaches, and you'll be getting a healthy dose of this important vitamin. The RDA is 1,000 International Units (IU).

VITAMIN B A whole slew of B vitamins help maintain a healthy nervous system and keep the brain functioning in the way that it should. B vitamins also contribute to good skin and hair, and may even be useful in treating depression. There are lots of ingredients to use in a smoothie that boost its B-vitamin content. Milk, fortified soy milk, peanut butter, avocados, and yogurt are just a few. The RDA for vitamin B6 is 2 mg and for vitamin B12 is 2.4 mcg (micrograms).

NUTRIENTS

glossary

VITAMIN C This powerful antioxidant detoxifies many harmful substances in the body and plays a key role in maintaining a healthy immune system. Vitamin C also promotes healthy gums and teeth, aids in iron absorption, maintains healthy connective tissue, and helps wounds to heal. Smoothies made with citrus fruits, strawberries, kiwis, or tomatoes will be rich in this essential vitamin. The RDA is 60 mg, although most health professionals recommend taking anywhere from 250 mg to 2,000 mg daily because it is such an effective antioxidant.

VITAMIN D Your body needs vitamin D in order to absorb and use calcium. Without it, bones and teeth cannot develop properly, and a deficiency of vitamin D may increase the risk of osteoporosis. Milk-based smoothies and those made with fortified soy milk are excellent sources of vitamin D. The RDA is 10mcg (micrograms) or 400 International Units (IU).

VITAMIN E Proper levels of vitamin E protect cells from oxidization. There's also evidence that it may reduce the risk of cardiovascular disease and inhibit the formation of clots in the arteries. Vitamin E is a powerful antioxidant that enhances immune response and may help prevent cataracts. For a vitamin-E rich smoothie, add peanut butter, sunflower seeds, avocado, mango, or flaxseed oil to the mix. The RDA is 8 mg a day for women and 10 mg a day for men, although most health professionals recommend getting anywhere from 100 to 400 mg daily because of vitamin E's strong antioxidant effects.

WATER Every single bodily function relies on water. It's what transports the nutrients in and the waste products out and keeps the digestive and circulatory tracts running smoothly. Water aids in weight loss and contributes to a good complexion as well. Smoothies, which are mostly water, are a fine way to ensure that your body gets all the H_2O it needs. Remember, the daily recommendation is eight to ten glasses of water a day.

a bit of advice:
preparing fruits and vegetables for smoothies

Smoothies are surely one of the simplest of all foods to prepare, but there are a few things to know that will make an easy task even easier. The most important thing to remember is that you can't make a good smoothie from bad produce. Shop carefully and choose the best your market has to offer.

Many of the recipes in this book call for fruits that are frozen. That's because frozen fruit helps make a cold smoothie that is thick and concentrated with fruit flavor. Fruit freezes quickly, most of it within a few hours, and having frozen fruit on hand means you can have a smoothie ready in just minutes.

Before freezing fruit, wash and dry it thoroughly. Peel the fruit if necessary, and then cut it into small pieces. Place the fruit flat in self-sealing plastic bags and freeze. For your convenience, you can also buy several kinds of frozen unsweetened fruit. We recommend that you use frozen fruit within two weeks.

What follows is a list of fruits and vegetables, with some notes on how to prepare them for smoothies. Please note that we don't recommend freezing vegetables for smoothies.

APPLES Peel, if desired, cut in half, and remove the core. Lay the apple flat-side down on a work surface and cut it into ½-inch pieces. Put in a self-sealing plastic bag and freeze if desired.

APRICOTS Cut in half and remove the pits. Lay the apricots, cut-side down, on a work surface and cut into ½-inch pieces. Put in a self-sealing plastic bag and freeze if desired. There are many different ways to hydrate dried apricots. We prefer the microwave method: Place the apricots in a small glass bowl and cover with water. Cover with plastic wrap and

PREPARATION

microwave for about 2 minutes on high power. Remove and let stand, covered, for 10 to 15 minutes, or until the water is absorbed. Drain if necessary. If you do not have a microwave, cover dried apricots with boiling water and soak for 10 to 15 minutes, or until soft. Drain before adding to smoothies.

BANANAS Peel bananas, put in a self-sealing plastic bag, and freeze if desired. Slice just before using.

BLACKBERRIES Sort through the berries, discarding any that are moldy or past their prime, and remove any stems. Rinse and place on a paper towel–lined tray. When dry, put the berries in a self-sealing plastic bag and freeze if desired.

BLUEBERRIES Sort through the berries, discarding any that are moldy or past their peak, and remove any stems. Rinse and place on a paper towel–lined tray. When dry, put the berries in a self-sealing plastic bag and freeze if desired.

CANTALOUPE Slice off both ends of the melon and put one end down on a work surface. Using a large knife, cut down the sides from top to bottom to remove the rind in thick strips, cutting around the contours of the melon. Cut the melon in half, scoop out the seeds, and cut the flesh into ½-inch pieces. Store in a sealed plastic container or in a self-sealing plastic bag. We don't recommend freezing cantaloupe because it doesn't retain enough of its already subtle flavor to create a flavor-packed smoothie.

CHERRIES Remove the stems. Rinse and place on a paper towel–lined tray. When dry, cut each cherry in half lengthwise, cutting around the pit, and pull the halves away from the pit. Alternately, pit the cherries with a cherry pitter. Put in a self-sealing plastic bag and freeze if desired.

CRANBERRIES Pour the berries into a large bowl of water. Sinkers are stinkers. Throw them out, along with any that are soft. Remove any stems. Dry cranberries on a paper towel–lined tray. Put in self-sealing plastic bags and freeze if desired.

DATES Remove the pits and chop the dates. If the dates are particularly hard, soak them in hot water for about 20 minutes, then drain before adding to smoothies. We do not recommend freezing dates.

GRAPEFRUIT Cut a thick slice off both ends of the fruit to reveal the flesh. Stand the grapefruit upright on a work surface. Using a large knife, cut down the sides of the fruit to remove the peel and the white pith in thick, wide strips, cutting around the contours of the fruit. Hold the peeled fruit over a bowl and carefully cut between the fruit and membrane on either side of each segment to free it. Discard the membrane (it can be very bitter and ruin the taste of a smoothie), along with any seeds. We do not recommend freezing grapefruit.

GRAPES Separate seedless grapes from their stems. Rinse and then put the grapes on a paper towel–lined tray. When dry, put in a self-sealing plastic bag and freeze if desired.

HONEYDEW MELON Cut a thick slice off both ends of the melon to reveal the flesh. Stand the fruit upright on a work surface. Using a large knife, cut down the sides of the melon to remove the rind in thick strips, cutting around the contours of the melon. Cut the melon in half and scoop out the seeds. We do not recommend freezing honeydew melon because it doesn't retain enough of its already subtle flavor to create a flavor-packed smoothie.

KIWIS With a sharp paring knife, cut a thick slice off both ends of the fruit to reveal the flesh. Stand the fruit upright on a work surface. Using a small knife, and working from top to bottom, cut off the brown skin in strips, cutting around the contours of the fruit. Cut the fruit into $\frac{1}{2}$-inch pieces. We do not recommend freezing kiwis.

MANGOS Cut a thick slice off both ends of the fruit to reveal the flesh. Stand the fruit upright on a work surface. Using a medium knife, cut down the sides of the mango to remove the skin in thin strips, cutting around the contours of the mango. Slice the fruit away from the long seed, and dice. Put the fruit in a self-sealing plastic bag and freeze if desired.

PREPARATION

NECTARINES Rinse and dry with a paper towel. Cut the fruit in half and remove the pit with a spoon. Then cut the fruit into ½-inch pieces. Put the fruit in a self-sealing plastic bag and freeze if desired.

ORANGES Cut a thick slice off both ends of the fruit to reveal the flesh. Stand the orange upright on a work surface. Using a medium knife, cut down the sides of the orange to remove the peel and the white pith in thick, wide strips, cutting around the contours of the fruit. Hold the peeled fruit over a bowl and carefully cut between the fruit and membrane on either side of each segment to free it. Discard the membrane (it can be very bitter and ruin the taste of a smoothie), along with any seeds. We do not recommend freezing oranges.

PAPAYAS Cut the fruit in half and scoop out the seeds. Cut off the peel with a paring knife and cut the fruit into ½-inch pieces. Put the fruit in a self-sealing plastic bag and freeze if desired.

PEACHES Peel the fruit, cut it in half, and remove the pit with a spoon. Then cut the fruit into ½-inch pieces or slices. Put the fruit in a self-sealing plastic bag and freeze if desired.

PINEAPPLE Cut a thick slice off the bottom and top of the pineapple. Set one end on a work surface. Using a large knife, cut down the sides from top to bottom, removing all the thick peel. Slice the fruit lengthwise into quarters, cut away the core, and chop the fruit into ½-inch pieces. Put the fruit in a self-sealing plastic bag and freeze if desired.

PLUMS Rinse and dry with a paper towel. Cut the plums in half, remove the pits with a spoon, and cut the fruit into ½-inch pieces. Put the fruit in a self-sealing plastic bag and freeze if desired.

PRUNES Prunes that have hardened should be plumped before adding to smoothies. Cover the fruit with boiling water and let stand for 10 minutes before draining. Be sure to remove any pits before using. We do not recommend freezing prunes.

RASPBERRIES Sort through the berries and discard any fruit that is moldy or spoiled. Rinse and place on a paper towel–lined tray. When dry, put the berries in a self-sealing plastic bag and freeze if desired.

STRAWBERRIES Rinse and place on a paper towel–lined tray. When dry, remove the green hulls from the fruit and cut the berries into quarters. Put them in a self-sealing plastic bag and freeze if desired.

WATERMELON Choose seedless watermelon, if possible. Cut the melon into quarters, remove any seeds, if necessary, and cut the red flesh away from the rind, then cut the flesh into ½-inch pieces. We do not recommend freezing watermelons.

AVOCADOS Slice the avocado in half lengthwise, cutting around the thick pit. Rotate the halves in opposite directions to separate them from the pit. Remove the pit and use a spoon to scoop the flesh out of the peel. Chop the flesh into small pieces. Avocados discolor quickly once exposed to the air. If not using immediately, sprinkle the flesh with a little lemon or lime juice to keep the color bright.

BEETS Peel raw beets with a vegetable peeler and remove the ends before grating. You may want to wear gloves to keep the juices from staining your hands. Grate on the largest holes of a four-sided hand grater.

CARROTS Peel carrots with a vegetable peeler and remove the ends before grating. Grate on the largest holes of a four-sided hand grater.

CUCUMBERS Rinse and pat dry with a paper towel. Cut cucumbers in half lengthwise and use a spoon to scrape out the seeds. Then chop the cucumber into small pieces. Because pesticides may be trapped under the wax coating found on some cucumbers, we recommend buying organic unwaxed cucumbers or shrink-wrapped English hothouse cucumbers.

RED BELL PEPPERS Rinse and pat dry with a paper towel. Cut the pepper in half lengthwise, scrape out the seeds and ribs, and remove the stem. Then chop the pepper into small pieces.

TOMATOES Rinse and pat dry with a paper towel. Use a paring knife to cut the core from the stem end of each tomato and chop the tomatoes coarsely into ½-inch pieces.

PREPARATION

information on
additives

Many juice and smoothie shops offer nutritional supplements that can be blended into your drinks. We believe, however, that the fresh-fruit blends in this book are brimming with healthy ingredients and that supplements are not necessary. The FDA has not evaluated the items on this list, and their benefits, if any, are unclear. Who knows? Maybe it's the placebo effect that has so many people hooked, or maybe it's all in the advertising. In time, more extensive studies will give us more conclusive evidence on these "wonder" potions. But for now, be aware that high doses and misuse of supplements can have serious side effects, so consult your health-care provider and educate yourself about supplements before you take them. Pregnant women, children, and anyone with a compromised immune system should consult their physician before taking any nutritional supplement. You should also know that these supplements can alter the taste and texture of a smoothie. So, just add a little to a small amount of a drink to test the effects before you add one to a blender full of smoothies.

ALGAE Due to excessive and effective marketing, algae products are popular additions to smoothies, spirulina and blue-green algae in particular. Algae tends to be easily digested, but the widespread claims that it is rich in protein, minerals, and vitamins are untrue. Be aware that these products have a saltwater flavor, so use them with caution at first.

BEE POLLEN This powderlike substance is what bees go about gathering as they fly from flower to flower. It may be useful for combating some of the effects of fatigue and depression, and it may also offer relief from allergies. Some people, though, are allergic to bee pollen, so if you are using it for the first time, start with a small amount to see whether a rash or other sign of allergic reaction develops.

BREWER'S YEAST Sometimes labeled nutritional yeast, brewer's yeast is grown on hops, the grain that's used for making beer. It's rich in

B vitamins, especially B12. Many people find that brewer's yeast gives them a boost of energy.

ECHINACEA This herb has gained popularity in recent years as an immune booster. Its supposed antimicrobial action may help prevent colds, flu, and other viral and bacterial infections, such as respiratory and urinary tract infections. Preliminary research shows that intake of this herb during the cold and flu season can reduce susceptibility to colds and flu, limit the duration and severity of infections, and fight recurrent infections. It is recommended to use it for no longer than eight weeks, followed by a one-week rest period before taking it again. Some health-care consultants caution against using echinacea prophylactically, and instead, advise its use only when you feel you are beginning to come down with a cold or flu. Echinacea may cause your tongue to tingle or to temporarily go numb, but this should be a harmless side effect.

GINGKO BILOBA Some studies suggest that this herb can help increase blood flow to the brain and may improve alertness, memory, and concentration. It can also function as a mood elevator, relieving both anxiety and dizziness, and it may also have benefits for those who suffer from asthma, allergies, bronchitis, and coughs. Watch your dosage carefully, though. In large amounts, gingko can cause diarrhea, irritability, and restlessness.

GINSENG In many parts of Asia, ginseng is revered as a tonic that can improve skin and muscle tone, and it is sometimes recommended to help strengthen those who are weakened by age or chronic illness. It may boost the immune system, help combat stress and fatigue, inhibit the growth of some cancer cells, and treat impotence and infertility. Some research suggests that high doses of ginseng may aid in the treatment of inflammatory diseases and that it may be useful to people with diabetes, by lowering blood sugar levels. Anyone with hypoglycemia, however, should avoid high amounts of ginseng, and no one, no matter what their health status, should take high doses of ginseng over a prolonged period of time. There are several distinct kinds of ginseng available; consult a book on supplements to find out which type you should take.

ADDITIVES

glossary

GOLDENSEAL This herb contains a substance considered by some to be a powerful antifungal and antibacterial compound and a natural antibiotic. Goldenseal is promoted as a useful agent for improving digestion, reducing blood pressure, and stimulating the central nervous system. Some people use it as a rinse to relieve cracked and bleeding lips, and canker sores. Pregnant women should be particularly cautious about using goldenseal, and anyone with glaucoma, diabetes, or heart disease should seek the advice of their doctor before they include this herb in their diet. Goldenseal is often combined with echinacea, as it is believed to boost that herb's effects.

GUTU KOLA This herb has a reputation as a longevity promoter. Some herbal-medicine advocates claim that gutu kola can relieve fatigue, depression, sleep disorders, and high blood pressure, and may even act as an aphrodisiac. There is currently no scientific evidence to support these claims.

HEMP SEED Don't get too excited. Yes, hemp is cannabis, the wild form of marijuana, but hemp is grown specifically for industrial and food use, and has virtually none of the intoxicating effects of its illicit cousin. There are a few other important differences between hemp and marijuana. One is that hemp seed can be bought in a natural foods store, rather than in a park downtown, and you don't get arrested. Also, hemp seed is one of the best-known sources of essential fatty acids and amino acids, necessary for everyday health and longevity. It has a light, nutty flavor that goes well with many smoothie blends.

KAVA A member of the pepper family, kava has been shown to reduce stress and nervousness, and to alleviate muscle aches and other chronic pain. Kava is thought to be a natural tranquilizer that relaxes the body and creates a calming effect. It has even been known to relieve insomnia, to prevent panic attacks, and to help relax some people who are afraid to fly. When purchasing kava, make sure that the label has at least 30 percent kavalactones, which are the herb's therapeutic ingredients. Take care not to use too high a dosage of this herb.

PROTEIN POWDER There are countless brands and flavors of protein powder on the market these days. We recommend soy protein powder because not only is it an excellent source of vegetable protein, but it offers many of the benefits of soy products as well. Evidence shows that soy protein powder promotes bone strength, thus helping to prevent osteoporosis. It can also aid in lowering cholesterol, thus helping to protect against heart disease. And soy protein powder has phytoestrogens which may help reduce hot flashes, one of the uncomfortable side effects of menopause.

WHEATGRASS JUICE You may have seen small cups of this vivid green juice at your natural foods store or juice bar. Touted as something of a nutritional powerhouse, it has been rumored that 2 ounces of fresh wheatgrass juice has as much nutritional value as 3 pounds of choice organic vegetables. Fans of wheatgrass juice claim that it is something of a cureall, helping to build blood, increase energy, cleanse the system, promote healing, and control weight, among other benefits.

ADDITIVES

energy elixirs

Exercise is a wonderful thing. It can give us energy, help us work more efficiently, and can facilitate weight loss and maintenance. The truth is, it also takes a toll on the body. To get the maximum benefit from any workout, it's vital to have the right fuel, and that's where smoothies can play an important role. Everyone who exercises needs two things: water and carbohydrates, ingredients with which fruit-rich smoothies are loaded.

The eight energy-rich smoothies in this chapter were developed specifically to enhance a workout. You'll find that they're not quite as thick as traditional smoothies. We made them thinner so they won't weigh you down and so your system can rapidly transport needed nutrients to the bloodstream.

Try the citrusy **ENERGIZER** before an early-morning run. When you're done, a carbohydrate-rich **RASPBERRY REFUELER** will replenish spent nutrients and aid in a speedy recovery. Fuel your body with **POWER PUNCH** before a killer bike ride or any-time fatigue threatens to sabotage your day. The tropical fruits in the **YOGA BLEND** are what you need if your goal is to be long and lean. Whether you're a marathoner, or just take an occasional aerobics class, there's a smoothie here to help you perform at your best.

power punch

This is a smoothie to sip when you return from the gym, a crucial time to replenish spent nutrients. The protein-rich tofu will give your brain a boost as it is rich in omega-3 fatty acids, which can guard against some of the negative effects of aging.

1/2 cup soft silken tofu
1 1/4 cups pear nectar
1/2 cup frozen diced pineapple
1/2 frozen banana, sliced
1 teaspoon fresh lime juice

Combine the tofu and pear nectar in a blender. Add all the remaining ingredients. Blend until smooth.

MAKES ABOUT 2 1/2 CUPS; SERVES 2

PER SERVING: calories 170; calories from fat 18 (10%); total fat 2 g; saturated fat 0.5 g; cholesterol 0 mg; carbohydrate 38 g; fiber 3 g; protein 3.5 g; vitamin A 39 i.u.; beta-carotene 0 mg; vitamin B6 0.2 mg; vitamin B12 0 mcg; vitamin C 11 mg; vitamin D 0 i.u.; vitamin E 0.2 mg; folate 12 mcg; calcium 30 mg; iron 1 mg; magnesium 35 mg; phosphorus 51 mg; potassium 281 mg; selenium 1 mcg; sodium 10 mg; phytochemicals: isoflavones, phenolic acids

the
energizer

Though it gets a bad rap, the truth is that for some people caffeine can have certain benefits. Many athletes swear that it's the secret to a great workout. We specifically like tea-based smoothies for workouts because they have half the caffeine of coffee, which means we get the jolt without the jitters. Tea is also less dehydrating than a cup of joe. The consistency of this smoothie is light and the taste is remarkably refreshing.

1 cup orange segments, chilled
½ cup grapefruit segments, chilled
½ cup strong-brewed Earl Grey tea, chilled
¾ cup orange sherbet
2 ice cubes, crushed

Combine the orange segments, grapefruit segments, and tea in a blender. Add the sherbet and ice. Blend until smooth.

MAKES ABOUT 2½ CUPS; SERVES 2

PER SERVING: calories 160; calories from fat 15 (9%); total fat 1.5 g; saturated fat 0.5 g; cholesterol 3.5 mg; carbohydrate 37 g; fiber 2.5 g; protein 2 g; vitamin A 310 i.u.; beta-carotene 0.2 mg; vitamin B6 0.1 mg; vitamin B12 0.1 mcg; vitamin C 70 mg; vitamin D 0 i.u.; vitamin E 0.4 mg; folate 40 mcg; calcium 82 mg; iron 0 mg; magnesium 21 mg; phosphorus 47 mg; potassium 334 mg; selenium 3 mcg; sodium 35 mg; caffeine 40 mg; phytochemicals: polyphenols, phenolic acids

raspberry
refueler

The two hours immediately after a workout are the optimal time to replace your body's carbohydrate stores, ideally within the first 15 minutes after you finish (this is when the enzymes responsible for making carbohydrates are most active). Raspberries help make this smoothie a great recovery drink for athletes. They're rich in nutrients, such as potassium, that are lost during exercise. We added Gatorade because it's a great way to replace carbohydrates and lost electrolytes, which regulate the flow of water across cell membranes.

1 cup diced mango
1 cup orange Gatorade
1 frozen banana, sliced
½ cup frozen unsweetened raspberries

Combine the mango and Gatorade in a blender. Add the banana and raspberries. Blend until smooth.

MAKES ABOUT 2 ½ CUPS; SERVES 2

PER SERVING: calories 151; calories from fat 5 (3%); total fat 0.5 g; saturated fat 0 g; cholesterol 0 mg; carbohydrate 39 g; fiber 4.5 g; protein 1 g; vitamin A 3,299 i.u; beta-carotene 2 mg; vitamin B6 0.5 mg; vitamin B12 0 mcg; vitamin C 36 mg; vitamin D 0 i.u.; vitamin E 1 mg; folate 35 mcg; calcium 19 mg; iron 0.5 mg; magnesium 31 mg; phosphorus 35 mg; potassium 415 mg; selenium 1 mcg; sodium 50 mg; phyto-chemicals: none

4 8

NOTE: This smoothie will separate after about 20
minutes; stir and it comes back together.

hydro-tonic

Despite what you may have heard, there are some good things
about sugar. A bit of it before you exercise can provide a burst of
energy to get your body going for strenuous exercise. Try this
smoothie during a workout to sustain endurance. Or, drink it 5
minutes before you begin exercising for a jolt of energy. You'll
also get 95 percent of your daily need for vitamin C!

1½ cups diced honeydew melon
1 cup lemon-lime Gatorade
¾ cup frozen green grapes
Pinch of salt

Combine the honeydew melon and Gatorade in a blender. Add
the grapes and salt. Blend until smooth. Serve immediately.

MAKES ABOUT 2½ CUPS; SERVES 2

PER SERVING: calories 112; calories from fat 5 (4%); total fat 0.5 g;
saturated fat 0 g; cholesterol 0 mg; carbohydrate 29 g; fiber 1 g; protein 1 g;
vitamin A 95 i.u.; beta-carotene 0.1 mg; vitamin B6 0.1 mg; vitamin B12 0 mcg; vitamin C 38 mg; vitamin D 0 i.u.; vitamin E 0.4 mg; folate 41 mcg; calcium 14 mg; iron
0.3 mg; magnesium 14 mg; phosphorus 21 mg; potassium 472 mg; selenium 6.5 mcg;
sodium 101 mg; phytochemicals: polyphenols

FECULE	RIZ	LIQUIDE
	400 Grs	1/2 LIT
400 Grs		45 Cl.
350 Grs	350 Grs	40 Cl.
300 Grs	300 Grs	35 Cl.
250 Grs	250 Grs	30 Cl.
200 Grs	200 Grs	1/4 LIT
150 Grs		20 Cl.
100 Grs	150 Grs	15 Cl.
75 Grs	100 Grs	10 Cl.
50 Grs	50 Grs	5 Cl.
HAFERFLOCKEN STARCH	REIS RICE	FLÜSSIGKEIT 1 POUND x 40cl

yoga blend

We're both big fans of Bikram method yoga, a type of yoga that combines an aerobic workout with the stretching and balancing poses of hatha yoga. During a Bikram-style practice, we work up quite a sweat, which costs us a lot of important minerals. This refreshing tropical-fruit smoothie restores lost nutrients and aids in the battle against fatigue.

1 1/2 cups quartered fresh strawberries
3/4 cup diced mango
3/4 cup chilled guava nectar
1/2 frozen banana, sliced
3 to 5 drops coconut extract (optional)

Combine the strawberries, mango, and guava nectar in a blender. Add the banana and optional coconut extract; blend until smooth.

MAKES ABOUT 2 1/2 CUPS; SERVES 2

PER SERVING: calories 160; calories from fat 9 (5%); total fat 1 g; saturated fat 0 g; cholesterol 0 mg; carbohydrate 40 g; fiber 5 g; protein 1.5 g; vitamin A 2,547 i.u.; beta-carotene 1.5 mg; vitamin B6 0.3 mg; vitamin B12 0 mcg; vitamin C 108 mg; vitamin D 0 i.u.; vitamin E 1 mg; folate 40 mcg; calcium 30 mg; iron 1 mg; magnesium 28 mg; phosphorus 40 mg; potassium 451 mg; selenium 1.5 mcg; sodium 5 mg; phytochemicals: beta-carotene, polyphenols, lycopene

vita pack

Carbohydrates are the preferred source of energy for working muscles, which is why it's so important to fuel up on them before a workout. This particular blend of yogurt and fruit has a whopping 53 grams of carbohydrates per serving. For the maximum benefit, drink it an hour or so before you exercise.

1 cup low-fat blueberry yogurt
¾ cup chilled apple juice
¾ cup fresh blueberries
1 cup frozen unsweetened chopped or sliced peaches

Combine the yogurt and apple juice in a blender. Add the blueberries and peaches and blend until smooth.

MAKES ABOUT 2½ CUPS; SERVES 2

PER SERVING: calories 238; calories from fat 12 (5%); total fat 1.5 g; saturated fat 0.5 g; cholesterol 9 mg; carbohydrate 53 g; fiber 3 g; protein 6 g; vitamin A 510 i.u.; beta-carotene 0.3 mg; vitamin B6 0.1 mg; vitamin B12 0.4 mcg; vitamin C 14 mg; vitamin D 0 i.u.; vitamin E 2 mg; folate 7 mcg; calcium 28 mg; iron 0.5 mg; magnesium 12 mg; phosphorus 158 mg; potassium 526 mg; selenium 1 mcg; sodium 65 mg; phytochemicals: beta-carotene

protein jolt

Protein helps balance blood sugar levels and is essential for repairing body tissue. This luscious smoothie is also rich in iron. We can't promise that you'll be able to run a marathon after you drink one of these, but it sure can't hurt.

> ¾ cup almond milk
> ½ cup plain low-fat yogurt
> ½ cup soft silken tofu
> ⅓ cup firmly packed chopped dates (about 8 dates),
> hydrated if necessary (see page 16)
> 2 tablespoons tahini or peanut butter
> 1 frozen banana, sliced

Combine the almond milk, yogurt, and tofu in a blender. Add all of the remaining ingredients and blend until smooth.

MAKES ABOUT 2½ CUPS; SERVES 2

PER SERVING: calories 311; calories from fat 116 (37%); total fat 12 g; saturated fat 2 g; cholesterol 5 mg; carbohydrate 46 g; fiber 5.5 g; protein 10 g; vitamin A 101 i.u.; beta-carotene 0.1 mg; vitamin B6 0.4 mg; vitamin B12 0.3 mcg; vitamin C 5 mg; vitamin D 0 i.u.; vitamin E 0.2 mg; folate 29 mcg; calcium 167 mg; iron 2 mg; magnesium 16 mg; phosphorus 254 mg; potassium 717 mg; selenium 1 mcg; sodium 78 mg; phytochemicals: isoflavones, phenolic acids

rejuvenator

Once your workout is over, reward yourself with this savory vegetable smoothie. It's absolutely delicious and a nice change of pace from the sweeter fruit-based drinks. We sometimes enjoy it as a quick lunch after a workout. It's just what we need to replenish spent carbohydrates, and it's rich in vitamin C to help repair damaged tissue. Canned tomatoes make a surprisingly wonderful smoothie. We don't use fresh tomatoes unless they are perfectly ripe at the absolute peak of the season.

> 1 cup canned diced tomatoes with juice
> 1/2 cup carrot juice, made into ice cubes and crushed
>   (see tips 4 and 5 on page 11)
> 1/2 cup soft silken tofu
> 1/2 cup chopped red bell peppers
> 1 tablespoon plus 2 teaspoons frozen orange juice
>   concentrate
> 1 teaspoon grated lemon zest
> 1/2 teaspoon Lawry's seasoned salt

Combine all the ingredients in a blender. Blend until smooth.

MAKES ABOUT 2 1/2 CUPS; SERVES 2

PER SERVING: calories 105; calories from fat 16 (15%); total fat 2 g; saturated fat 0 g; cholesterol 0 mg; carbohydrate 20 g; fiber 3 g; protein 4 g; vitamin A 16,830 i.u.; beta-carotene 10 mg; vitamin B6 0.4 mg; vitamin B12 0 mcg; vitamin C 96 mg; vitamin D 0 i.u.; vitamin E 1 mg; folate 52 mcg; calcium 42 mg; iron 1.5 mg; magnesium 41 mg; phosphorus 94 mg; potassium 657 mg; selenium 1 mcg; sodium 563 mg; phytochemicals: beta-carotene, isoflavones, lycopene, phenolic acids, terpenes

immune boosters

When we're sick or feeling under the weather, smoothies are our food of first defense. We drink them to help prevent illness and aid in a quick recovery when we do come down with a bug. Eating solid food is sometimes difficult when you're ill, but it's important to get the nutrients your body needs to heal. That's when a tall, cool smoothie can come to the rescue.

At the first sign of a cold, sip on a **C-BREEZE** to get a mega-dose of this important vitamin. The gingery **STOMACH SOOTHER** can help calm an upset tummy, while the **BETA BOOST** may help guard against more serious diseases. We don't promise any cures in this chapter, just eight great-tasting smoothies that can contribute to your well-being.

Stomach Soother ➤

flu-buster

The combination of orange juice, papaya, and strawberries gives this terrific smoothie a triple dose of vitamin C. It's custom-made for those stuffy-head, runny-nose, feeling-lousy kind of days. Take one before bedtime and hopefully there'll be no need to call the doctor in the morning.

> 1 cup fresh orange juice
> 1 cup quartered fresh strawberries
> ¾ cup diced papaya
> 1 frozen banana, sliced

Combine the orange juice and strawberries in a blender. Add the papaya and banana. Blend until smooth.

MAKES ABOUT 2½ CUPS; SERVES 2

PER SERVING: calories 174; calories from fat 9 (5%); total fat 1 g; saturated fat 0 g; cholesterol 0 mg; carbohydrate 42 g; fiber 6 g; protein 3 g; vitamin A 337 i.u.; beta-carotene 0.2 mg; vitamin B6 0.5 mg; vitamin B12 0 mcg; vitamin C 171 mg; vitamin D 0 i.u.; vitamin E 1 mg; folate 112 mcg; calcium 48 mg; iron 1 mg; magnesium 49 mg; phosphorus 62 mg; potassium 844 mg; selenium 2 mcg; sodium 5 mg; phytochemicals: carotenoids, phenolic acids, lycopene

c-breeze

The combination of kiwi and cantaloupe offers a whopping 230 percent of the RDA for vitamin C, along with 80 percent of the RDA for vitamin A. That combination could mean death to your next cold. This smoothie tastes delightfully similar to the Sweet Tart candies we loved as kids. If your kiwis are really ripe and sweet (and not very tart), you may want to add a squeeze of fresh lime juice.

1 cup diced kiwi (about 3), chilled
1 cup orange sherbet
1¾ cups diced cantaloupe, chilled

Combine all the ingredients in a food processor. Process until smooth.

MAKES ABOUT 2½ CUPS; SERVES 2

PER SERVING: calories 251; calories from fat 25 (10%); total fat 3 g; saturated fat 1 g; cholesterol 5 mg; carbohydrate 58 g; fiber 3.5 g; protein 3.5 g; vitamin A 4,786 i.u.; beta-carotene 3 mg; vitamin B6 0.3 mg; vitamin B12 0 mcg; vitamin C 175 mg; vitamin D 0 i.u.; vitamin E 0.5 mg; folate 53 mcg; calcium 97 mg; iron 1 mg; magnesium 57 mg; phosphorus 108 mg; potassium 903 mg; selenium 3 mcg; sodium 63 mg; phytochemicals: beta-carotene

heart throb

If you're one of the 13.5 million Americans who have a history of heart disease, this smoothie is for you. Berries are rich in polyphenols, which may reduce the risk of heart disease. There's a hefty dose of potassium, too, which may also help reduce high blood pressure.

½ cup apricot nectar
¾ cup low-fat boysenberry yogurt
¾ cup chopped nectarines
¾ cup frozen unsweetened blackberries
4 ice cubes, crushed

Combine the apricot nectar, yogurt, and nectarines in a blender. Add the blackberries and crushed ice and blend until smooth.

MAKES ABOUT 2½ CUPS; SERVES 2

PER SERVING: calories 195; calories from fat 18 (9%); total fat 2 g; saturated fat 0.5 g; cholesterol 6 mg; carbohydrate 43 g; fiber 5 g; protein 5 g; vitamin A 1,620 i.u.; beta-carotene 1 mg; vitamin B6 0.1 mg; vitamin B12 0 mcg; vitamin C 38 mg; vitamin D 0 i.u.; vitamin E 1 mg; folate 22 mcg; calcium 158 mg; iron 1 mg; magnesium 21 mg; phosphorus 31 mg; potassium 526 mg; selenium 1 mcg; sodium 60 mg; phytochemicals: polyphenols, beta-carotene

fountain of
youth

Cherries, blueberries, and cranberries are all fantastic sources of vitamin C and anthocyanins, antioxidants that may protect against some types of cancer. Vitamin C supports the growth of strong collagen fibers in soft connective tissue and bone which may help prevent some of the ravages of age. Enjoyed on a regular basis, this smoothie just may be one of the secrets to staying young.

1 cup low-fat cherry yogurt
¼ cup cranberry juice
1 cup frozen pitted cherries
¾ cup frozen unsweetened blueberries

Combine the yogurt and cranberry juice in a blender. Add the cherries and berries. Blend until smooth.

MAKES ABOUT 2½ CUPS; SERVES 2

PER SERVING: calories 230; calories from fat 20 (8%); total fat 2 g; saturated fat 1 g; cholesterol 8 mg; carbohydrate 49 g; fiber 3 g; protein 5 g; vitamin A 211 i.u.; beta-carotene 0.1 mg; vitamin B6 0.1 mg; vitamin B12 0.5 mcg; vitamin C 23 mg; vitamin D 0 i.u.; vitamin E 2 mg; folate 7 mcg; calcium 165 mg; iron 0.5 mg; magnesium 11 mg; phosphorus 145 mg; potassium 431 mg; selenium 1 mcg; sodium 59 mg; phytochemicals: polyphenols, terpenes

14-carrot

This creamy blend of carrots and orange juice is chock-full of beta-carotene, which can help fortify a weakened immune system. Soy products such as tofu are in the forefront of foods believed to help prevent disease. They're loaded with phytochemicals, powerful compounds that are thought to protect the body from cancer and other illnesses as well. So don't wait any longer to drink this liquid gold!

½ cup soft silken tofu
½ cup chilled carrot juice
½ cup grated carrots
1 cup low-fat vanilla frozen yogurt
2 tablespoons frozen orange juice concentrate
1 tablespoon fresh lemon juice
¼ teaspoon grated fresh ginger
Pinch of salt
3 tablespoons pumpkin seeds (optional)

Combine the tofu, carrot juice, and grated carrots in a blender. Add the frozen yogurt, orange juice concentrate, lemon juice, ginger, and salt. Blend until smooth. Add the pumpkin seeds, if you like, and blend to the desired consistency.

MAKES ABOUT 2½ CUPS; SERVES 2

PER SERVING: calories 294; calories from fat 63 (21%); total fat 7 g; saturated fat 2 g; cholesterol 50 mg; carbohydrate 47 g; fiber 4 g; protein 13 g; vitamin A 23,632 i.u.; beta-carotene 14 mg; vitamin B6 0.2 mg; vitamin B12 0 mcg; vitamin C 35 mg; vitamin D 0 i.u.; vitamin E 1 mg; folate 35 mcg; calcium 244 mg; iron 2 mg; magnesium 51 mg; phosphorus 238 mg; potassium 705 mg; selenium 1 mcg; sodium 148 mg; phytochemicals: beta-carotene, phenolic acids, isoflavones

stomach
soother

A tall glass of this comforting smoothie can help tame an out-of-sorts tummy. Ginger has been prescribed for centuries as an antidote for nausea. The combination of fresh fruits and green tea makes a surprisingly refreshing drink.

¾ cup strong-brewed green tea, chilled
1 cup diced apricots
¾ cup mango sorbet
2 tablespoons frozen pineapple juice concentrate
1 teaspoon fresh lime juice
¼ teaspoon grated fresh ginger

Combine the green tea and apricots in a blender. Add all the remaining ingredients and blend until smooth.

MAKES ABOUT 2½ CUPS; SERVES 2

PER SERVING: calories 153; calories from fat 5 (3%); total fat 0.5 g; saturated fat 0 g; cholesterol 0 mg; carbohydrate 37 g; fiber 3.5 g; protein 2 g; vitamin A 3,107 i.u.; beta-carotene 2 mg; vitamin B6 0.1 mg; vitamin B12 0 mcg; vitamin C 67 mg; vitamin D 0 i.u.; vitamin E 1 mg; folate 23 mcg; calcium 25 mg; iron 1 mg; magnesium 21 mg; phosphorus 33 mg; potassium 522 mg; selenium 0 mcg; sodium 7 mg; phytochemicals: beta-carotene, phenolic acids, polyphenols

scale-tipper
sipper

Some folks with compromised immune systems have a hard time keeping weight on. We made this high-calorie smoothie just for them. We included lots of fresh mango, which is full of beta-carotene and potassium, both necessary for a healthy immune system. If you're in the mood for fun, add a splash of rum and turn this smoothie into a tropical cocktail.

> ⅓ cup unsweetened coconut milk
> 1 cup low-fat vanilla yogurt
> 1½ cups diced mango
> 1 frozen banana, sliced
> 1 tablespoon fresh lime juice

Combine the coconut milk and yogurt in a blender. Add all the remaining ingredients. Blend until smooth.

MAKES ABOUT 2½ CUPS; SERVES 2

PER SERVING: calories 318; calories from fat 90 (28%); total fat 10 g; saturated fat 8 g; cholesterol 10 mg; carbohydrate 55 g; fiber 5 g; protein 7 g; vitamin A 4,916 i.u.; beta-carotene 3 mg; vitamin B6 0.5 mg; vitamin B12 0.6 mcg; vitamin C 42 mg; vitamin D 0 i.u.; vitamin E 1.5 mg; folate 40 mcg; calcium 198 mg; iron 2 mg; magnesium 45 mg; phosphorus 211 mg; potassium 749 mg; selenium 2 mcg; sodium 75 mg; phytochemicals: beta-carotene, phenolic acids

beta boost

The yellow or orange color of a fruit or vegetable is a clue that it's rich in beta-carotene, which is what the body uses to make vitamin A. It's an important nutrient with all sorts of great benefits, like protection against memory loss, heart disease, cancer, and stroke. Of course those same fruits and vegetables make an excellent smoothie, which is really why we like them so much.

1 cup diced mango
1 cup chilled carrot juice
1 cup frozen unsweetened quartered strawberries
⅓ cup chopped red bell pepper

Combine the mango and carrot juice in a blender. Add the strawberries and bell pepper. Blend until smooth.

MAKES ABOUT 2½ CUPS; SERVES 2

PER SERVING: calories 132; calories from fat 9 (7%); total fat 1 g; saturated fat 0 g; cholesterol 0 mg; carbohydrate 32 g; fiber 5 g; protein 2 g; vitamin A 35,849 i.u.; beta-carotene 22 mg; vitamin B6 0.5 mg; vitamin B12 0 mcg; vitamin C 112 mg; vitamin D 0 i.u.; vitamin E 2 mg; folate 39 mcg; calcium 51 mg; iron 1 mg; magnesium 35 mg; phosphorus 80 mg; potassium 655 mg; selenium 2 mcg; sodium 39 mg; phytochemicals: beta-carotene, phenolic acids, polyphenols, lycopene

weight-conscious
concoctions

Smoothies are a wonderful food for people watching their waistlines. Not only is it simple to make them low in calories, but you can also load them with the important nutrients that many folks miss out on when they're eating lightly.

Because smoothies are fruit-based, they are naturally rich in carbohydrates, which some researchers believe can help decrease appetite and combat depression—two things that can sabotage a weight-loss regimen.

The six smoothies here are nutritious low-calorie drinks that have been formulated to help you drop a few pounds. They're filling, full of flavor, and low in fat and calories. When you're facing a powerful craving for something rich and sweet, satisfy it with a glass of **GUILTLESS PLEASURE.** It tastes like pure indulgence, even though it has just 160 calories per serving. **PEACHY LEAN** makes a terrific low-fat breakfast. It's rich in energy-giving carbohydrates to get the day off to a good start. And a luscious **LEAN 'N GREEN** is the perfect midday snack.

skinny minnie

Honeydew and cantaloupe have hardly any calories, and yet they're full of flavor and nutrition, two things that anyone, whether they're watching their weight or not, can appreciate. The orange-fleshed cantaloupe is a good source of vitamin A and beta-carotene, which can help guard against heart disease and stroke.

> 2 cups diced cantaloupe
> ⅓ cup lemon sorbet
> 2 teaspoons frozen orange juice concentrate
> 1 teaspoon fresh lemon juice
> 4 ice cubes, crushed
> Pinch of salt

Combine all the ingredients in a blender. Blend until smooth.

MAKES ABOUT 2 CUPS; SERVES 2

PER SERVING: calories 134; calories from fat 5 (4%); total fat 0.5 g; saturated fat 0 g; cholesterol 0 mg; carbohydrate 33 g; fiber 2 g; protein 2 g; vitamin A 21,000 i.u.; beta-carotene 13 mg; vitamin B6 0.3 mg; vitamin B12 0 mcg; vitamin C 88 mg; vitamin D 0 i.u.; vitamin E 0.3 mg; folate 39 mcg; calcium 34 mg; iron 0.5 mg; magnesium 28 mg; phosphorus 57 mg; potassium 717 mg; selenium 1 mcg; sodium 33 mg; phytochemicals: beta-carotene, phenolic acids

guiltless
pleasure

Tofu, soy milk, and bananas give this terrific smoothie a rich, luscious texture. You'll think you're drinking a milkshake, when in fact this drink contains just 160 calories and only 2.5 grams of fat! Pineapples and strawberries boost the vitamin-C content, which helps to prevent hardening of the arteries.

1 cup quartered fresh strawberries
½ cup light vanilla soy milk
⅓ cup soft silken tofu
1 frozen banana, sliced
2 tablespoons frozen pineapple juice concentrate

Combine the strawberries, soy milk, and tofu in a blender. Add the banana and pineapple concentrate. Blend until smooth.

MAKES ABOUT 2 CUPS; SERVES 2

PER SERVING: calories 160; calories from fat 21 (13%); total fat 2.5 g; saturated fat 0.5 g; cholesterol 0 mg; carbohydrate 33 g; fiber 3 g; protein 4.5 g; vitamin A 82 i.u.; beta-carotene 0 mg; vitamin B6 0.4 mg; vitamin B12 0 mcg; vitamin C 60 mg; vitamin D 0 i.u.; vitamin E 0.4 mg; folate 32 mcg; calcium 49 mg; iron 1 mg; magnesium 43 mg; phosphorus 60 mg; potassium 525 mg; selenium 1.5 mcg; sodium 5 mg; phytochemicals: isoflavones, lycopene, polyphenols

peachy lean

Skipping breakfast is a serious mistake if you're trying to lose weight. A morning meal jump-starts the metabolism, giving your body the fuel it needs in order to get going after a night's sleep. And calories consumed throughout the day are more likely to be burned for energy than stored for fat. This irresistible blend of peach and blackberries will get your motor running with a burst of antioxidants and a minimum of fat.

½ cup low-fat peach yogurt
¼ cup unsweetened apple juice
1 cup frozen unsweetened blackberries
½ cup frozen unsweetened chopped or sliced peaches
1 frozen banana, sliced

Combine the yogurt and apple juice in a blender. Add all the remaining ingredients. Blend until smooth. Strain through a fine-meshed sieve to remove the blackberry seeds if you like.

MAKES ABOUT 2 CUPS; SERVES 2

PER SERVING: calories 186; calories from fat 9 (5%); total fat 1 g; saturated fat 0.5 g; cholesterol 5 mg; carbohydrate 43 g; fiber 5 g; protein 4 g; vitamin A 393 i.u.; beta-carotene 0.2 mg; vitamin B6 0.4 mg; vitamin B12 0.2 mcg; vitamin C 25 mg; vitamin D 0 i.u.; vitamin E 2.5 mg; folate 37 mcg; calcium 99 mg; iron 1 mg; magnesium 35 mg; phosphorus 102 mg; potassium 592 mg; selenium 2 mcg; sodium 31 mg; phytochemicals: polyphenols

constant cravings

Cravings often spell doom for anyone trying to lose a few pounds, but it doesn't have to be that way. When you just can't go another minute without something creamy and sweet, this delicious and rich-tasting smoothie will satisfy without the calories and fat that can do you in. Don't peel the apple if you're looking for extra fiber in your diet.

> ¾ cup low-fat vanilla yogurt
> ¾ cup diced apple, peeled or unpeeled
> ½ cup apple juice, made into ice cubes and crushed
> (see page 11)
> ½ frozen banana, sliced
> Pinch of ground cardamom, cinnamon, or nutmeg

Combine the yogurt and apples in a blender. Add all the remaining ingredients. Blend until smooth.

MAKES ABOUT 2 CUPS; SERVES 2

PER SERVING: calories 162; calories from fat 13 (8%); total fat 1.5 g; saturated fat 1 g; cholesterol 7.5 mg; carbohydrate 35 g; fiber 1.5 g; protein 4 g; vitamin A 83 i.u.; beta-carotene 0.1 mg; vitamin B6 0.2 mg; vitamin B12 0.5 mcg; vitamin C 6 mg; vitamin D 0 i.u.; vitamin E 0.5 mg; folate 7 mcg; calcium 140 mg; iron 0.5 mg; magnesium 12 mg; phosphorus 125 mg; potassium 414 mg; selenium 0.5 mcg; sodium 53 mg; phytochemicals: none

lite 'n luscious

If your weight-loss regimen includes exercise, this is a smoothie for you. Not only are raspberries extremely low in calories but they're also a source of potassium, which is often lost during exercise.

¾ cup quartered fresh strawberries
¾ cup unsweetened apple juice
½ cup frozen unsweetened raspberries
1 frozen banana, sliced

Combine all the ingredients in a blender. Blend until smooth.

MAKES ABOUT 2 CUPS; SERVES 2

PER SERVING: calories 136; calories from fat 5 (3%); total fat 0.5 g; saturated fat 0 g; cholesterol 0 mg; carbohydrate 34 g; fiber 5 g; protein 1.5 g; vitamin A 115 i.u.; beta-carotene 0.1 mg; vitamin B6 0.4 mg; vitamin B12 0 mcg; vitamin C 44 mg; vitamin D 0 i.u.; vitamin E 0.5 mg; folate 32 mcg; calcium 28 mg; iron 1 mg; magnesium 35 mg; phosphorus 31 mg; potassium 496 mg; selenium 2 mcg; sodium 8 mg; phytochemicals: lycopene, polyphenols

lean 'n green

There are few foods quite as refreshing as melon, and combined with frozen green grapes, the result is uniquely clean and satisfying. The addition of cucumber in this smoothie makes it cool and hydrating, certain to be welcome on a sweltering summer day. Even those who aren't counting their calories and fat grams will be wowed by this healthy version of a green slurpee.

1½ cups chopped honeydew melon, chilled
½ cup white grape juice
½ cup chopped seeded cucumber
¾ cup frozen green grapes

Combine the honeydew, grape juice, and cucumber in a blender. Add the grapes. Blend until smooth.

MAKES ABOUT 2 CUPS; SERVES 2

PER SERVING: calories 109; calories from fat 5 (4%); total fat 0.5 g; saturated fat 0 g; cholesterol 0 mg; carbohydrate 28 g; fiber 1 g; protein 1 g; vitamin A 155 i.u.; beta-carotene 0.1 mg; vitamin B6 0.2 mg; vitamin B12 0 mcg; vitamin C 87 mg; vitamin D 0 i.u.; vitamin E 0.5 mg; folate 44 mcg; calcium 23 mg; iron 0.5 mg; magnesium 15 mg; phosphorus 31 mg; potassium 506 mg; selenium 10 mcg; sodium 16 mg; phytochemicals: polyphenols

for the gals

Women are blessed with a complicated system of hormones that yields great rewards, such as children and an increased life expectancy. However, most of us must deal with a few problems that are not so fun, such as menstrual cramps, morning sickness, and hot flashes. Fortunately, the amount of attention paid to women's health issues has increased dramatically in recent years, and as a result nutritionists now have all sorts of information and recommendations for women's unique nutritional needs. This chapter takes advantage of that research and offers some smoothies developed just for women.

When Mary was pregnant, she found relief in our **MORNING-SICKNESS SOLUTION** and got her daily dose of important nutrients with the **MATERNITY MEDLEY.** Because many women need extra iron in their diet, we came up with **ADIOS ANEMIA.** The calcium-rich **BONE BUILDER** provides protection against our increased risk of osteoporosis. And while we're not really looking forward to the days when hot flashes become a problem, we'll be ready to cool down with a tall glass of **COLD FLASH.**

Bone Builder ➤

cold flash

Soy foods like tofu and soy milk are rich in phytoestrogens, which can act in much the same way that natural estrogen does. This is good news for menopausal women, who may find that an estrogen boost can relieve hot flashes and some of the other discomforts associated with this time of life.

> 2 tablespoons dried apricots (about 6)
> ¼ cup water
> ½ cup soft silken tofu
> 1 cup light vanilla soy milk
> 1 cup frozen unsweetened chopped or sliced peaches
> ¾ cup peach sorbet

Put the apricots in a small glass bowl or short-rimmed glass with the water. Cover with plastic wrap and microwave for 2 minutes on high power. Remove and let stand, covered, for 10 to 15 minutes until the water is absorbed. Or, pour boiling water over the apricots, cover with plastic wrap, and let stand, covered, until tender. Combine the tofu, soy milk, and apricots in a blender. Add the peaches and sorbet. Blend until smooth.

MAKES ABOUT 2½ CUPS; SERVES 2

PER SERVING: calories 214; calories from fat 25 (11%); total fat 3 g; saturated fat 0.5 g; cholesterol 0 mg; carbohydrate 44 g; fiber 4 g; protein 7 g; vitamin A 1,238 i.u.; beta-carotene 1 mg; vitamin B6 0.1 mg; vitamin B12 0 mcg; vitamin C 5 mg; vitamin D 0 i.u.; vitamin E 0.6 mg; folate 5 mcg; calcium 60 mg; iron 1 mg; magnesium 30 mg; phosphorus 71 mg; potassium 406 mg; selenium 1 mcg; sodium 44 mg; phytochemicals: beta-carotene, isoflavones

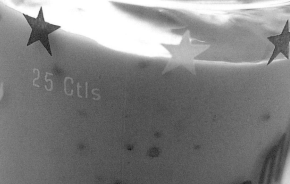

pms potion

It may be hard to believe that this indulgent blend of chocolate and raspberries is good for you, but it's true. There's evidence that chocolate can stimulate the pleasure centers in the brain—not that we need a scientist to tell us that! And soy contains plant-based hormones that can help relieve some of the mood swings that sometimes accompany PMS. Fresh mint is not only the perfect garnish, but it may also help reduce cramps.

¾ cup chocolate soy milk
1¼ cups frozen unsweetened raspberries
½ banana, sliced
¾ cup chocolate sorbet
2 tablespoons chopped fresh mint

Combine the soy milk, raspberries, and banana in a blender. Add the sorbet and mint. Blend until smooth.

MAKES ABOUT 2½ CUPS; SERVES 2

PER SERVING: calories 229; calories from fat 23 (10%); total fat 2.5 g; saturated fat 1 g; cholesterol 0 mg; carbohydrate 49 g; fiber 7 g; protein 6 g; vitamin A 128 i.u.; beta-carotene 0.1 mg; vitamin B6 0.2 mg; vitamin B12 0 mcg; vitamin C 22 mg; vitamin D 0 i.u.; vitamin E 0.1 mg; folate 26 mcg; calcium 20 mg; iron 1 mg; magnesium 22 mg; phosphorus 15 mg; potassium 230 mg; selenium 1 mcg; sodium 31 mg; phytochemicals: isoflavones

bone builder

The flavor of this smoothie reminds us of a raspberry Julius, that juice drink we loved as kids. We were thrilled to find out that raspberries, which are one of our favorite fruits, help prevent chronic disease. When the raspberries are combined with the bone-building calcium found in yogurt, milk, and powdered milk, they make one mighty smoothie. Be aware that boosting your calcium intake on a regular basis may prevent osteoporosis.

1 cup low-fat raspberry yogurt
¾ cup low-fat milk
1 cup frozen unsweetened quartered strawberries
½ cup frozen unsweetened raspberries
⅓ cup powdered milk

Combine the yogurt and low-fat milk in a blender. Add all the remaining ingredients. Blend until smooth.

MAKES ABOUT 2½ CUPS; SERVES 2

PER SERVING: calories 250; calories from fat 32 (13%); total fat 3.5 g; saturated fat 2 g; cholesterol 16.5 mg; carbohydrate 44 g; fiber 3.5 g; protein 8 g; vitamin A 515 i.u.; beta-carotene 0.8 mg; vitamin B6 0.1 mg; vitamin B12 1.2 mcg; vitamin C 56 mg; vitamin D 86 i.u.; vitamin E 0.2 mg; folate 33 mcg; calcium 283 mg; iron 1 mg; magnesium 40 mg; phosphorus 342 mg; potassium 727 mg; selenium 6 mcg; sodium 163 mg; phytochemicals: lycopene

NOTE: This smoothie can be made 1 day before serving.
It can also be served in a bowl and eaten with a spoon. Try garnishing
it with basil or mint for a complementary flavor twist.

87

maternity
medley

When Mary was pregnant, she was constantly looking for ways to make sure she was getting all the nutrients necessary for a healthy baby. This delicious blend was often her lunch. It tastes something like a rich gazpacho and has plenty of vitamins to satisfy a growing babe.

> One 14¼-ounce can diced tomatoes with juice
> ½ cup low-fat lemon yogurt
> ½ cup chopped avocado
> 2 tablespoons tomato paste
> ½ teaspoon balsamic vinegar
> 1 teaspoon celery salt
> Dash of Tabasco
> 2 to 4 ice cubes, crushed

Combine all the ingredients in a blender. Blend until smooth.

MAKES ABOUT 2½ CUPS; SERVES 2

PER SERVING: calories 171; calories from fat 64 (37%); total fat 7 g; saturated fat 1.5 g; cholesterol 5 mg; carbohydrate 25 g; fiber 4 g; protein 6 g; vitamin A 1,903 i.u.; beta-carotene 1.2 mg; vitamin B6 0.4 mg; vitamin B12 0.4 mcg; vitamin C 41 mg; vitamin D 0 i.u.; vitamin E 2 mg; folate 43 mcg; calcium 151 mg; iron 2 mg; magnesium 48 mg; phosphorus 142 mg; potassium 949 mg; selenium 1.5 mcg; sodium 504 mg; phytochemicals: beta-carotene, lycopene

8 8

NOTE: For variety, we like to add a drop of orange oil, which gives this smoothie a surprising depth of flavor. Or, try adding 2 tablespoons flaxseed oil or ground flaxseed for essential fatty acids.

adios
anemia

Iron deficiency is one of the most common nutritional problems in America, and one that particularly affects women. To make matters more difficult, only a small portion of the iron we eat is actually absorbed by our bodies, so we need to consume a lot just to get a little. Prunes, we're happy to report, are an excellent source of this important nutrient and they make a smoothie that is absolutely over-the-top in flavor.

½ cup low-fat vanilla yogurt

1 cup vanilla soy milk

⅓ cup diced pitted prunes, rehydrated if necessary (see page 20)

1 frozen banana, sliced

2 to 4 ice cubes, crushed

Combine the yogurt and soy milk in a blender. Add all the remaining ingredients. Blend until smooth.

MAKES ABOUT 2½ CUPS; SERVES 2

PER SERVING: calories 313; calories from fat 25 (8%); total fat 3 g; saturated fat 0.5 g; cholesterol 5 mg; carbohydrate 69 g; fiber 6.5 g; protein 7.5 g; vitamin A 1,198 i.u.; beta-carotene 0.7 mg; vitamin B6 0.5 mg; vitamin B12 0.3 mcg; vitamin C 7 mg; vitamin D 0 i.u.; vitamin E 1.5 mg; folate 13 mcg; calcium 143 mg; iron 2 mg; magnesium 42 mg; phosphorus 131 mg; potassium 905 mg; selenium 2 mcg; sodium 79 mg; phytochemicals: isoflavones

NOTE: Drink this smoothie right away, before the natural
pectins in the blueberries cause it to congeal.

honeymooner's
tonic

For years, women have told one another about the miracle cure for
bladder infections: cranberry juice. Research has confirmed that
the berries do contain a chemical that can help prevent one of the
symptoms of what's sometimes called "honeymooner's disease."
Blueberries contain the same chemical and are rich, too, in pain-
relieving compounds that can reduce inflammation.

1 cup cranberry juice
1 cup fresh blueberries
1 frozen banana, sliced
½ cup strawberry sorbet

Combine all the ingredients in a blender. Blend until smooth.

MAKES ABOUT 2½ CUPS; SERVES 2

PER SERVING: calories 220; calories from fat 9 (4%); total fat 1 g; saturated fat 0
g; cholesterol 0 mg; carbohydrate 55 g; fiber 3 g; protein 1 g; vitamin A 124 i.u.;
beta-carotene 0.1 mg; vitamin B6 0.4 mg; vitamin B12 0 mcg; vitamin C 63 mg; vitamin D 0 i.u.; vitamin E 2 mg; folate 16 mcg; calcium 12 mg; iron 0.5 mg; magnesium
23 mg; phosphorus 21 mg; potassium 343 mg; selenium 1 mcg; sodium 15 mg; phytochemicals: polyphenols

morning-sickness
solution

The queasiness that often accompanies pregnancy can make it difficult to eat, which means that pregnant women sometimes miss out on important nutrients. Ginger, which has been prescribed for centuries to calm uneasy stomachs, lends this delicious blend of peaches and pears a mildly spicy flavor. It's a terrific breakfast for expectant moms.

> 1½ cups diced pears
> ½ cup low-fat peach yogurt
> ½ cup pear nectar
> 1 teaspoon fresh lemon juice
> ¼ teaspoon grated fresh ginger
> 3 to 5 ice cubes, crushed

Combine the pears, peach yogurt, and pear nectar in a blender. Add all the remaining ingredients. Blend until smooth.

MAKES ABOUT 2½ CUPS; SERVES 2

PER SERVING: calories 194; calories from fat 7 (3%); total fat 1 g; saturated fat 0 g; cholesterol 4 mg; carbohydrate 46 g; fiber 3 g; protein 3 g; vitamin A 12 i.u.; beta-carotene 0 mg; vitamin B6 0 mg; vitamin B12 0.2 mcg; vitamin C 5 mg; vitamin D 0 i.u.; vitamin E 0 mg; folate 4 mcg; calcium 95 mg; iron 1 mg; magnesium 15 mg; phosphorus 87 mg; potassium 293 mg; selenium 0.5 mcg; sodium 38 mg; phytochemicals: phenolic acids

kid shakes and baby blends

The birth of Mary's son, Jackson, has been a wonderful introduction to parenthood for us. Not only has the little guy increased our awareness of pediatric nutrition, but he has also made us realize that smoothies are a perfect food for kids. Smoothies are not only easy to eat, but they're also packed with important vitamins and nutrients essential for growing up healthy—and most importantly, kids love them.

When Jackson was just a babe in arms, we gave him a **BRAIN POWER** smoothie for some added nutrients as well as a little variety in his diet. When his first teeth arrived, Mary developed **PLUM TEETHIN'**, an icy cold smoothie to soothe his sore gums. As he's grown, we've found that smoothies are a great way to give Jackson nutritional foods that aren't filled with refined sugar and artificial ingredients.

This chapter includes some of Jackson's favorite smoothies as well as some others that we're looking forward to packing in his lunch box in the years ahead.

Brain Power ➤

school-bus
breakfast

Researchers and nutritionists know that kids who eat breakfast perform better in school than those who don't, but parents know that getting kids to eat a healthy morning meal is not always easy. Well, you'll hear no excuses when this eye-opening blend of strawberries and bananas is served. It takes only a few minutes to make and drink, and it's rich in vitamin C and protein. Plus, kids find it irresistible.

1 cup low-fat vanilla yogurt
½ cup strawberry nectar
¾ cup frozen unsweetened quartered strawberries
1 frozen banana, sliced

Combine the yogurt and strawberry nectar in a blender. Add the strawberries and banana. Blend until smooth.

MAKES ABOUT 2½ CUPS; SERVES 2

PER SERVING: calories 210; calories from fat 18 (8%); total fat 2g; saturated fat 1g; cholesterol 10 mg; carbohydrate 44 g; fiber 2 g; protein 6g; vitamin A 113 i.u.; beta-carotene 0.1 mg; vitamin B6 0.4 mg; vitamin B12 0.6 mcg; vitamin C 42 mg; vitamin D 0 i.u.; vitamin E 0.5 mg; folate 22 mcg; calcium 187 mg; iron 0.5 mg; magnesium 23 mg; phosphorus 173 mg; potassium 595 mg; selenium 1 mcg; sodium 75 mg; phytochemicals: lycopene, polyphenols

plum teethin'

(6 MONTHS AND OLDER)

When Mary's little boy, Jackson, began to get his first teeth, we developed this icy cold smoothie to soothe his pain. It's rich in Vitamin C to ensure that teeth grow in healthy and strong. This fruit combination will delight any baby that may be bored with the somewhat limited variety of fruits available in jars.

¾ cup diced cantaloupe
⅓ cup frozen diced unpeeled plums
⅓ cup frozen pitted cherries

Put the cantaloupe in a blender. Add the plums and cherries. Blend until smooth.

MAKES ABOUT 1 CUP; SERVES 2

PER SERVING: calories 75; calories from fat 9 (12%); total fat 1 g; saturated fat 0 g; cholesterol 0 mg; carbohydrate 18 g; fiber 2 g; protein 1.5 g; vitamin A 2,163 i.u.; beta-carotene 1 mg; vitamin B6 0.1 mg; vitamin B12 0 mcg; vitamin C 33 mg; vitamin D 0 i.u.; vitamin E 1 mg; folate 13 mcg; calcium 15 mg; iron 0.5 mg; magnesium 14 mg; phosphorus 23 mg; potassium 354 mg; selenium 1 mcg; sodium 5 mg; phyto-chemicals: beta-carotene, terpenes

over the rainbow

When we were kids, rainbow sherbet, a blend of orange, lime, and raspberry, was the dessert we loved best. We've re-created the flavors of that childhood favorite here in a healthy blend of juice and fruit that's better for us than the sherbet we consumed as youngsters.

1 cup orange segments
¾ cup chilled apple juice
1 cup orange sherbet
1 cup frozen unsweetened raspberries

Combine the orange segments and apple juice in a blender. Add the sherbet and raspberries. Blend until smooth.

MAKES ABOUT 2½ CUPS; SERVES 2

PER SERVING: calories 249; calories from fat 22 (9%); total fat 2.5g; saturated fat 1g; cholesterol 5 mg; carbohydrate 58 g; fiber 4 g; protein 2.5 g; vitamin A 338 i.u; beta-carotene 0.2 mg; vitamin B6 0.2 mg; vitamin B12 0.1 mcg; vitamin C 68 mg; vitamin D 0 i.u.; vitamin E 0.2 mg; folate 47 mcg; calcium 108 mg; iron 1 mg; magnesium 31 mg; phosphorus 65 mg; potassium 459 mg; selenium 3 mcg; sodium 47 mg; phytochemicals: phenolic acids

grape
escape

Kids flip for this vivid purple smoothie. It's a terrific way to get a juice fix, and because it's made with yogurt, it's rich in calcium, which is essential for strong bones and teeth.

> 1 cup low-fat vanilla frozen yogurt
> 1/2 cup grape juice
> 3/4 cup frozen red grapes
> 3/4 cup frozen unsweetened blueberries

Combine the frozen yogurt and grape juice in a blender. Add the grapes and blueberries. Blend until smooth.

MAKES ABOUT 2 1/2 CUPS; SERVES 2

PER SERVING: calories 299; calories from fat 45 (15%); total fat 5 g; saturated fat 2 g; cholesterol 50 mg; carbohydrate 58 g; fiber 2 g; protein 11 g; vitamin A 122 i.u.; beta-carotene 0.1 mg; vitamin B6 0.2 mg; vitamin B12 0 mcg; vitamin C 17 mg; vitamin D 0 i.u.; vitamin E 1 mg; folate 9 mcg; calcium 213 mg; iron 1 mg; magnesium 14 mg; phosphorus 170 mg; potassium 439 mg; selenium 9 mcg; sodium 57 mg; phytochemicals: polyphenols

NOTE: This smoothie will thicken as it sits, due to the pectins in the blueberries. Babies enjoy the thicker consistency as well.

breakfast
on the crawl

(6 MONTHS AND OLDER)

Every parent knows that getting breakfast down a wiggly kid can be quite a feat. Mary solved the problem by combining some of Jackson's favorite foods in this delicious smoothie. Some babies may have an allergic reaction to strawberries. If your little one has never had them, introduce a very small amount at first and wait for up to five days to see if an allergic reaction happens.

½ cup breast milk or formula
⅓ cup quartered fresh strawberries
⅓ cup fresh blueberries
½ banana, sliced
About ¼ cup dry rice baby cereal

Put the milk or formula in a blender. Add the strawberries, blueberries, and banana. Blend until smooth. Add rice cereal to the desired consistency.

MAKES ABOUT 1 CUP; SERVES 2

PER SERVING: calories 99; calories from fat 20 (20%); total fat 2 g; saturated fat 1 g; cholesterol 4 mg; carbohydrate 20 g; fiber 2 g; protein 1.5 g; vitamin A 129 i.u.; beta-carotene 0.2 mg; vitamin B6 0.2 mg; vitamin B12 0 mcg; vitamin C 23 mg; vitamin D 1 i.u.; vitamin E 1 mg; folate 14 mcg; calcium 62 mg; iron 2.5 mg; magnesium 13 mg; phosphorus 43 mg; potassium 196 mg; selenium 1 mcg; sodium 7 mg; phytochemicals: polyphenols, lycopene

NOTE: Doctors and nutritionists do not recommend feeding low-fat products to babies or children under the age of 2. Infants need fat in order for their brains to develop properly. Use whole-milk yogurt when making smoothies for little ones.

101

brain power

(6 MONTHS AND OLDER)

Babies love the sweet, peachy taste of this smoothie. We added flaxseed oil because it contains fatty acids that are essential for brain development. This wholesome fruit medley, made without refined sugar, is perfect for young palates.

½ cup plain whole-milk yogurt
½ cup frozen unsweetened chopped or sliced peaches
2 tablespoons frozen apple juice concentrate
½ teaspoon flaxseed oil

Combine all the ingredients in a blender. Blend until smooth.

MAKES ABOUT 1 CUP; SERVES 2

PER SERVING: calories 88; calories from fat 16 (18%); total fat 1.5 g; saturated fat 0.5 g; cholesterol 5 mg; carbohydrate 16 g; fiber 1 g; protein 3 g; vitamin A 253 i.u.; beta-carotene 0.2 mg; vitamin B6 0 mg; vitamin B12 0.3 mcg; vitamin C 3 mg; vitamin D 0 i.u.; vitamin E 0.5 mg; folate 2 mcg; calcium 106 mg; iron 0 mg; magnesium 6 mg; phosphorus 85 mg; potassium 292 mg; selenium 1 mcg; sodium 42 mg; phytochemicals: omega-3 fatty acids

after-school
snack attack

Welcome your little Einstein home from school with a tall glass of this chocolatey smoothie. Inspired by old-fashioned rocky road sundaes, it's a nutritious way to top off a birthday party or celebrate the victory of your favorite soccer team.

½ cup soft silken tofu
¾ cup chilled chocolate rice milk
½ cup chocolate sorbet
1 frozen banana, sliced
¼ cup toasted pecans (optional)
¼ cup miniature marshmallows (optional)

Combine the tofu and rice milk in a blender. Add the sorbet and banana. Blend until smooth. Add the pecans and marshmallows, if you like, and blend to the desired consistency.

MAKES ABOUT 2½ CUPS; SERVES 2

PER SERVING: calories 300; calories from fat 87 (29%); total fat 10 g; saturated fat 1g; cholesterol 0 mg; carbohydrate 51 g; fiber 4 g; protein 6 g; vitamin A 63 i.u.; beta-carotene 0 mg; vitamin B6 0.4 mg; vitamin B12 0 mcg; vitamin C 6 mg; vitamin D 0 i.u.; vitamin E 0.5 mg; folate 15 mcg; calcium 130 mg; iron 1 mg; magnesium 44 mg; phosphorus 75 mg; potassium 362 mg; selenium 1 mcg; sodium 48 mg; phytochemicals: isoflavones, phenolic acids

fellows for the

Our husbands, Erik and Jack, are big smoothie hounds. Though they aren't enthusiastic about cooking, they are always keen to flip the switch on a fruit-filled blender. Like us, they enjoy them almost every day. This chapter is full of smoothies not just for them, but for all the guys who want to maintain their vitality.

There has been some remarkable nutritional research done in the field of male infertility. Some studies even reveal that certain foods may increase the odds of conception. We've used some of the findings to develop smoothies that may help give birth to a new generation of smoothie-lovers.

The **LIBIDO LIFTER** may spark a little romance, and if conception is your goal, a **VIRILITY VIBE** might just increase your odds. If it's a son that you desire, **DR. SHETTLES'S SECRET** could be the key, and men looking to add a bit more bulk to their frame will enjoy the peanut butter–based **INCREDIBLE HULK.**

libido lifter

This sexy smoothie is perfect for sharing with your sweetie. Chocolate has long been valued as an aphrodisiac, and researchers have found that it does contain chemicals that stimulate the pleasure centers of the brain. The little bit of vanilla extract here may also have a stimulating effect on the nerves responsible for sexual response. So dim the lights and drink up.

1 cup low-fat chocolate milk
½ cup chocolate sorbet
2 frozen bananas, sliced
2 tablespoons toasted almonds (optional)
2 teaspoons vanilla extract

Combine the milk and sorbet in a blender. Add the bananas and blend until smooth. Add the almonds, if using, and the vanilla. Blend to the desired consistency.

MAKES ABOUT 2½ CUPS; SERVES 2

PER SERVING: calories 335; calories from fat 74 (22%); total fat 8 g; saturated fat 3 g; cholesterol 8.5 mg; carbohydrate 59 g; fiber 7 g; protein 9 g; vitamin A 343 i.u.; beta-carotene 0.5 mg; vitamin B6 1 mg; vitamin B12 0.5 mcg; vitamin C 12 mg; vitamin D 50 i.u.; vitamin E 10 mg; folate 32 mcg; calcium 177 mg; iron 1 mg; magnesium 50 mg; phosphorus 151 mg; potassium 724 mg; selenium 4 mcg; sodium 77 mg; phytochemicals: isoflavones, phenolic acids

virility vibe

When it's time to think about producing an heir, future fathers might want to start adding more vitamin E to their diet. This decadent smoothie is spiked with peanuts and wheat germ, vitamin-E rich ingredients. There's evidence that this vitamin can increase the chances of conception. Some researchers believe this wonder vitamin has libido-enhancing properties.

$\frac{1}{2}$ cup vanilla soy milk
$\frac{1}{2}$ cup low-fat vanilla yogurt
1 frozen banana, sliced
2 tablespoons lightly salted peanuts
2 tablespoons wheat germ
2 tablespoons old-fashioned oats
2 teaspoons maple syrup
6 to 8 ice cubes, crushed

Combine the soy milk and yogurt in a blender. Add the banana. Blend until smooth. Add all the remaining ingredients and blend to the desired consistency.

MAKES ABOUT 2 $\frac{1}{2}$ CUPS; SERVES 2

PER SERVING: calories 260; calories from fat 66 (25%); total fat 7.5 g; saturated fat 1.5 g; cholesterol 5 mg; carbohydrate 42 g; fiber 3.5 g; protein 10 g; vitamin A 76 i.u.; beta-carotene 0.1 mg; vitamin B6 0.4 mg; vitamin B12 0.3 mcg; vitamin C 6 mg; vitamin D 0 i.u.; vitamin E 3.5 mg; folate 49 mcg; calcium 120 mg; iron 1.5 mg; magnesium 64 mg; phosphorus 238 mg; potassium 574 mg; selenium 9 mcg; sodium 96 mg; phytochemicals: isoflavones, phenolic acids

dr. shettles's
secret

Some of the most exciting discoveries in fertility research come from Dr. Landrum B. Shettles, a man whom *Omni* magazine named one of the twentieth century's titans in the field. One of the more interesting things that the doctor has found is that men who consume a relatively high dose of caffeine just before intercourse have an increased chance of producing a son. So if it's a boy you're hoping for, you may want to give this smoothie a try. Note that long-term use of caffeine may reduce sperm count, so don't overdo it. Also, caffeine is not recommended for women who are trying to conceive.

> ¾ cup low-fat cherry yogurt
> ½ cup cold strong-brewed coffee
> ¾ cup low-fat chocolate frozen yogurt
> 1½ cups frozen pitted cherries

Combine the cherry yogurt and coffee in a blender. Add the frozen yogurt and cherries. Blend until smooth.

MAKES ABOUT 2½ CUPS; SERVES 2

PER SERVING: calories 304; calories from fat 45 (15%); total fat 5 g; saturated fat 2 g; cholesterol 36 mg; carbohydrate 56 g; fiber 2 g; protein 10 g; vitamin A 282 i.u.; beta-carotene 0.2 mg; vitamin B6 0 mg; vitamin B12 0.3 mcg; vitamin C 8 mg; vitamin D 0 i.u.; vitamin E 1 mg; folate 5 mcg; calcium 239 mg; iron 1 mg; magnesium 14 mg; phosphorus 225 mg; potassium 606 mg; selenium 1.5 mcg; sodium 76 mg; caffeine 30 mg; phytochemicals: terpenes

the incredible hulk

If you think tofu is for sissies, think again. Sumo wrestlers don't get that big eating sushi. Tofu is a great way to get the calories needed to build muscles. It's also rich in anti-aging antioxidants and can help reduce cholesterol levels, as well.

½ cup soft silken tofu
¾ cup low-fat milk
2 tablespoons peanut butter
2 frozen bananas, sliced
1 teaspoon honey

Combine the tofu and milk in a blender. Add all the remaining ingredients. Blend until smooth.

MAKES ABOUT 2½ CUPS; SERVES 2

PER SERVING: calories 287; calories from fat 110 (38%); total fat 12 g; saturated fat 3 g; cholesterol 7 mg; carbohydrate 39 g; fiber 4 g; protein 11 g; vitamin A 665 i.u; beta-carotene 0.4 mg; vitamin B6 0.8 mg; vitamin B12 0.3 mcg; vitamin C 11 mg; vitamin D 37 i.u.; vitamin E 2 mg; folate 38 mcg; calcium 142 mg; iron 1 mg; magnesium 88 mg; phosphorus 207 mg; potassium 806 mg; selenium 6 mcg; sodium 125 mg; phytochemicals: isoflavones, phenolic acids

reducers stress

Planning parties for a living has taught us a little bit about stress. Not only do we have to deal with our own hectic schedules, but part of our job as caterers is to soothe the nerves of jittery hosts and excitable mothers of brides. Stress takes a tremendous toll on our body, depleting it of essential nutrients. It can also be linked to many serious health problems, including heart disease and cancer. Since we can't afford to let stress threaten our busy life, we make sure to take care of ourselves, and that includes drinking lots of smoothies.

The recipes in this chapter are ones that we rely on when stress threatens to sabotage our health. A glass of the chamomile tea–based **SLEEPY TEA** just before bed helps send us sweetly off to dreamland so that we can get the rest we need. After a particularly crazy day, a tropical **TENSION TAMER** helps us relax and make the transition from work to home. And the fruity **CHOLESTEROL CLEANSER** protects against some of the risks of high blood pressure and heart disease, which increase with stress. So, drink up and chill out.

NOTE: Drained mandarin oranges work well in place of the
orange segments if you are in a hurry, or if you are craving this smoothie
in the middle of the summer when oranges are not in season.

115

sleepy tea

Russian tea, one of our favorite drinks when we were kids growing up in North Carolina, provided the inspiration for this comforting smoothie. The spicy blend of oranges, cloves, and tea is
wonderfully soothing, especially when made with chamomile.
Caffeine-free and oh-so relaxing, chamomile also aids in digestion, so the effects of a big meal no longer keep us awake at night.

1½ cups orange segments
2 tablespoons frozen orange juice concentrate
1 tablespoon fresh lemon juice
2 teaspoons honey
2 pinches ground cinnamon
Pinch of ground cloves
1 cup strong-brewed chamomile tea, made into ice cubes
  and crushed (see page 11)

Combine the orange segments, orange concentrate, lemon juice,
honey, cinnamon, and cloves in a blender. Blend until the mixture
is smooth and the honey is dissolved. Add the crushed tea ice
cubes and blend until smooth.

MAKES ABOUT 2½ CUPS; SERVES 2

PER SERVING: calories 117; calories from fat 2 (2%); total fat 0 g; saturated fat 0
g; cholesterol 0 mg; carbohydrate 30 g; fiber 3 g; protein 2 g; vitamin A 352 i.u; beta-
carotene 0.2 mg; vitamin B6 0.1 mg; vitamin B12 0 mcg; vitamin C 100 mg; vitamin
D 0 i.u.; vitamin E 0.5 mg; folate 70 mcg; calcium 64 mg; iron 0.5 mg; magnesium 22
mg; phosphorus 30 mg; potassium 389 mg; selenium 1.5 mcg; sodium 2; phytochemicals: phenolic acids

116

NOTE: Fresh litchis are difficult to find and are available only a few months a year. We like the convenience of canned litchis. Look for them in Asian markets.

tension
tamer

We know that rum is not a cure for stress, but when taken in moderation it can help relieve some of the tensions of a busy day. Of course, you can leave the rum out and this tropical smoothie will still taste great. You'll also enjoy the benefits of mango, a fruit rich in nutrients that can help promote a strong immune system. Litchi nuts lend this smoothie an aromatic, exotic flavor, and they're a good source of vitamin C, an antioxidant that protects against the effects of stress. For those who are opposed to a little booze, substitute rum flavoring for a great alternative.

½ cup unsweetened light coconut milk
⅓ cup light rum
¼ cup litchi syrup
1 cup canned litchi nuts, drained, chopped, and frozen
1 cup frozen chopped mango
1 tablespoon fresh lime juice
6 to 8 ice cubes, crushed

Combine the coconut milk, rum, and litchi syrup in a blender. Add all the remaining ingredients. Blend until smooth.

MAKES ABOUT 2½ CUPS; SERVES 2

PER SERVING: calories 297; calories from fat 50 (17%); total fat 5.5 g; saturated fat 3 g; cholesterol 0 mg; carbohydrate 42 g; fiber 2.5 g; protein 1.5 g; vitamin A 3,213 i.u.; beta-carotene 2 mg; vitamin B6 0.2 mg; vitamin B12 0 mcg; vitamin C 62 mg; vitamin D 0 i.u.; vitamin E 1 mg; folate 35 mcg; calcium 31 mg; iron 4 mg; magnesium 16 mg; phosphorus 34 mg; potassium 251 mg; selenium 0 mcg; sodium 4; phytochemicals: phenolic acids, beta-carotene

stress buster

One of our favorite ways to relax is to slip out onto the deck and sip this soothing smoothie cocktail. Inspired by the popular Sea Breeze, this drink is healthier. It is full of fiber and beta-carotene that you wouldn't get from the average cocktail. This unforgettable concoction is tart and tangy and perfect for taking the edge off a rough day.

¾ cup cranberry-tangerine juice
⅓ cup vodka
2 cups frozen unsweetened chopped or sliced peaches
2 tablespoons frozen pineapple juice concentrate

Combine the cranberry juice and vodka in a blender. Add the peaches and pineapple juice concentrate. Blend until smooth.

MAKES ABOUT 2½ CUPS; SERVES 2

PER SERVING: calories 232; calories from fat 3 (1%); total fat 0.5 g; saturated fat 0 g; cholesterol 0 mg; carbohydrate 39 g; fiber 3 g; protein 1.5 g; vitamin A 1,051 i.u.; beta-carotene 0.6 mg; vitamin B6 0.1 mg; vitamin B12 0 mcg; vitamin C 51 mg; vitamin D 0 i.u.; vitamin E 2 mg; folate 14 mcg; calcium 23 mg; iron 0.5 mg; magnesium 22 mg; phosphorus 33 mg; potassium 487 mg; selenium 2.5 mcg; sodium 3mg; phytochemicals: polyphenols, phenolic acids

cholesterol cleanser

Stress can wreak havoc on cholesterol levels and increase the like-
lihood of heart disease. This smoothie, inspired by our favorite
sangría, is based on research that indicates that moderate alcohol
consumption may play a role in a heart-healthy diet. Blackberries
add a great flavor to the mix and are rich in antioxidants, which
may help to reduce the risk of coronary disease.

¾ cup fruity red wine, such as Zinfandel or Pinot Noir
⅓ cup frozen apple juice concentrate
1½ cups frozen pitted cherries
½ cup frozen unsweetened blackberries

Combine the wine and apple juice concentrate in a blender. Add
the cherries and blackberries. Blend until smooth.

MAKES ABOUT 2½ CUPS; SERVES 2

PER SERVING: calories 292; calories from fat 5 (2%); total fat 0.5 g; saturated fat
0 g; cholesterol 0 mg; carbohydrate 57 g; fiber 5 g; protein 2 g; vitamin A 289 i.u.;
beta-carotene 0.2 mg; vitamin B6 0.1 mg; vitamin B12 0 mcg; vitamin C 9 mg; vitamin D 0 i.u.; vitamin E 1 mg; folate 15 mcg; calcium 47 mg; iron 4 mg; magnesium 42
mg; phosphorus 32 mg; potassium 624 mg; selenium 1 mcg; sodium 26; phytochemicals: polyphenols, terpenes

our faves

We've created hundreds of smoothies over the past few years and are often asked to name our favorite. Well, that would be impossible. There are just too many fabulous fruit combinations. Every time we think we've found the best of the best, we discover a new blend that's even better. So instead of picking just one great smoothie, we decided to include six that top our list.

The soothing **HANGOVER HELPER,** made with watermelon and lots of fresh strawberries, is so refreshing that we enjoy it even if we haven't over-indulged the night before. An intriguing combination of fruits and vegetables makes **CAN'T BEET IT!** one unbeatable lunchtime smoothie. We enjoy it several times a week and never grow tired of it. And just one sip of the creamy **PEACH PIZZAZZ** takes us right back to our grandmother's kitchen and the summers we spent growing up in North Carolina. There's no way we could pick just one smoothie as our favorite. The truth is, we love them all.

Minty Fresh & Peach Pizzazz ➤

fiber burst

Bananas and dates are a wonderful combination that's made even better when tangy, creamy buttermilk is added to the mix. This is a terrific breakfast smoothie. Try pouring over Grapenuts for an ultra-satisfying start (in this case, delete the ice cubes). If your dates have hardened, cover them with boiling water and let stand for 15 minutes before draining. This smoothie tends to be thick, so if you prefer a looser consistency, thin with milk.

½ cup low-fat maple yogurt
⅔ cup buttermilk
⅓ cup pitted dates (about 8 dates), coarsely chopped, rehydrated if necessary (see page 16)
2 frozen bananas, sliced
2 tablespoons bran
2 to 3 ice cubes, crushed

Combine the yogurt and buttermilk in a blender. Add all the remaining ingredients. Blend until smooth.

MAKES ABOUT 2½ CUPS; SERVES 2

PER SERVING: calories 286; calories from fat 23 (8%); total fat 2.5 g; saturated fat 1 g; cholesterol 6 mg; carbohydrate 65 g; fiber 5.5 g; protein 8.5 g; vitamin A 167 i.u.; beta-carotene 0.2 mg; vitamin B6 0.8 mg; vitamin B12 0.5 mcg; vitamin C 12 mg; vitamin D 3 i.u.; vitamin E 0.5 mg; folate 39 mcg; calcium 219 mg; iron 1 mg; magnesium 76 mg; phosphorus 233 mg; potassium 936 mg; selenium 7 mcg; sodium 129mg; phytochemicals: none

late-night snack attack

This is an extraordinary smoothie that's rich in energy-fueling carbohydrates and is a good source of potassium, too. The tropical fruit flavor is astonishingly intense and, with the addition of coconut milk, it easily earns the status of pure indulgence. Sip it slowly and be transported to an island paradise.

> ½ cup unsweetened light coconut milk
> 1 ¼ cups diced fresh pineapple
> 1 frozen banana, sliced
> ¾ cup passion fruit sorbet

Combine the coconut milk and pineapple in a blender. Add the banana and sorbet. Blend until smooth.

MAKES ABOUT 2 ½ CUPS; SERVES 2

PER SERVING: calories 206; calories from fat 52 (25%); total fat 6 g; saturated fat 3 g; cholesterol 0 mg; carbohydrate 39 g; fiber 2.5 g; protein 2.5 g; vitamin A 69 i.u.; beta-carotene 0 mg; vitamin B6 0.4 mg; vitamin B12 0 mcg; vitamin C 20 mg; vitamin D 0 i.u.; vitamin E 0 mg; folate 35 mcg; calcium 30 mg; iron 4 mg; magnesium 31 mg; phosphorus 18 mg; potassium 337 mg; selenium 1.5 mcg; sodium 36mg; phytochemicals: none

hangover helper

We throw parties for a living, so we know a little about hangovers. We've learned that what your body really craves when you wake up with a pounding head and a parched mouth is water. Watermelon is approximately 92 percent water and an excellent electrolyte replacer.

> 2 cups diced seeded watermelon
> 1 cup frozen unsweetened quartered strawberries
> ¼ cup raspberry sorbet
> 2 teaspoons fresh lime juice
> Pinch of salt

Combine the watermelon and strawberries in a blender. Add all the remaining ingredients and blend until smooth.

MAKES ABOUT 2½ CUPS; SERVES 2

PER SERVING: calories 109; calories from fat 7 (6%); total fat 1 g; saturated fat 0 g; cholesterol 0 mg; carbohydrate 26 g; fiber 2.5 g; protein 1.5 g; vitamin A 622 i.u.; beta-carotene 0.4 mg; vitamin B6 0.3 mg; vitamin B12 0 mcg; vitamin C 48 mg; vitamin D 0 i.u.; vitamin E 0.5 mg; folate 17 mcg; calcium 25 mg; iron 1 mg; magnesium 26 mg; phosphorus 25 mg; potassium 302 mg; selenium 2 mcg; sodium 7 mg; phytochemicals: lycopene, phenolic acids

peach pizzazz

We won't go on and on about how rich in beta-carotene, potassium, and vitamin C this smoothie is. Instead, we'll just say that it's as close as you can get to a fresh peach cobbler without turning on your oven. Serve it with a couple of ginger crisps and see for yourself.

1 cup low-fat peach yogurt
½ cup low-fat evaporated milk
1 cup frozen unsweetened chopped or sliced peaches
½ cup peach sorbet
¼ teaspoon ground cinnamon
Pinch of ground allspice

Combine the yogurt and evaporated milk in a blender. Add all the remaining ingredients. Blend until smooth.

MAKES ABOUT 2½ CUPS; SERVES 2

PER SERVING: calories 255; calories from fat 24 (9%); total fat 2.5 g; saturated fat 1.5 g; cholesterol 13 mg; carbohydrate 49 g; fiber 2 g; protein 10 g; vitamin A 740 i.u.; beta-carotene 0.8 mg; vitamin B6 0.1 mg; vitamin B12 0.6 mcg; vitamin C 6 mg; vitamin D 0 i.u.; vitamin E 1 mg; folate 8 mcg; calcium 338 mg; iron 0.5 mg; magnesium 23 mg; phosphorus 256 mg; potassium 581 mg; selenium 2 mcg; sodium 150 mg; phytochemicals: none

minty fresh

This delightful hydrating smoothie tastes like summer to us.
Rich in potassium, which works to control the body's balance of
water, it's a refreshing antidote to a sun-baked afternoon. A mea-
sure of fresh mint lends flavor, and works as a breath freshener
after a garlicky meal.

1 ½ cups diced honeydew melon
½ cup low-fat lemon yogurt
1 cup frozen green grapes
1 tablespoon chopped fresh mint
Fresh lemon juice to taste (optional)

Combine the honeydew melon and lemon yogurt in a blender.
Add the grapes and mint. Blend until smooth. Taste and add
lemon juice if you like.

MAKES ABOUT 2 ½ CUPS; SERVES 2

PER SERVING: calories 157; calories from fat 12 (7%); total fat 1.5 g; saturated fat
0.5 g; cholesterol 5 mg; carbohydrate 36 g; fiber 1 g; protein 4 g; vitamin A 135 i.u.;
beta-carotene 0.1 mg; vitamin B6 0.2 mg; vitamin B12 0.3 mcg; vitamin C 42 mg; vitamin D 0 i.u.; vitamin E 0.5 mg; folate 42 mcg; calcium 105 mg; iron 0.5 mg; magnesium 14 mg; phosphorus 98 mg; potassium 614 mg; selenium 8.5 mcg; sodium
49mg; phytochemicals: polyphenols, phenolic acids

can't beet it!

Beets might seem like an odd ingredient for a smoothie, but paired with the right fruits and vegetables, they create a wonderful earthiness that is not overpowering. Loaded with natural sugars and powerful disease-fighting antioxidants, they make a vivid smoothie that's gorgeous to behold.

¼ cup grated raw beet
¾ cup carrot juice
¾ cup apple juice
1½ cups frozen diced papaya
2 teaspoons fresh lime juice
¼ teaspoon grated fresh ginger

Combine the beets, carrot juice, and apple juice in a blender. Add all the remaining ingredients and blend until smooth.

MAKES ABOUT 2½ CUPS; SERVES 2

PER SERVING: calories 133; calories from fat 4 (3%); total fat 0.5 g; saturated fat 0 g; cholesterol 0 mg; carbohydrate 32 g; fiber 3 g; protein 2 g; vitamin A 24,062 i.u.; beta-carotene 14 mg; vitamin B6 0.3 mg; vitamin B12 0 mcg; vitamin C 76 mg; vitamin D 0 i.u.; vitamin E 0.5 mg; folate 61 mcg; calcium 58 mg; iron 1 mg; magnesium 32 mg; phosphorus 59 mg; potassium 721 mg; selenium 1 mcg; sodium 49 mg; phytochemicals: beta-carotene, phenolic acids, lycopene

index

table of equivalents

The exact equivalents in the following tables have been rounded for convenience.

abbreviations

US / UK	METRIC
oz=ounce	g=gram
lb=pound	kg=kilogram
in=inch	mm=millimeter
ft=foot	cm=centimeter
tbl=tablespoon	ml=milliliter
fl oz=fluid ounce	l=liter
qt=quart	

length measures

⅛ in	3 mm
¼ in	6 mm
½ in	12 mm
1 in	2.5 cm

weights

US/UK	METRIC
1 oz	30 g
2 oz	60 g
3 oz	90 g
4 oz (¼ lb)	125 g
5 oz (⅓ lb)	155 g
6 oz	185 g
7 oz	220 g
8 oz (½ lb)	250 g
10 oz	315 g
12 oz (¾ lb)	375 g
14 oz	440 g
16 oz (1 lb)	500 g
1½ lb	750 g
2 lb	1 kg
3 lb	1.5 kg

liquids

US	METRIC	UK
2 tbl	30 ml	1 fl oz
¼ cup	60 ml	2 fl oz
⅓ cup	80 ml	3 fl oz
½ cup	125 ml	4 fl oz
⅔ cup	160 ml	5 fl oz
¾ cup	180 ml	6 fl oz
1 cup	250 ml	8 fl oz
1½ cups	375 ml	12 fl oz
2 cups	500 ml	16 fl oz